THE
IMPACTORS

The Impactors

Copyright © 2019 Vicky Omifolaji

All rights reserved.

ISBN: 978-0-244-20514-0

All rights reserved. No part of this book may be reproduced or transmitted in any form without prior permission in writing from the publisher.

DISCLAIMER: This book is designed to motivate and encourage readers. The methods described in this book represent the author's personal experiences. They are not intended to be a definitive set of instructions for each individual. They are intended to be used as a guide only, and represent only the author's personal belief.

Dedication

The Impactors is dedicated to the Future Generation of Women Impactors.

Honouring all the Beautiful Powerful women that came before us.

Foreword

Women today are told that they are strong, but the top of governments and industries around the world today are still stubbornly male.

We have come a long way in a short time as women. It was August 26, 1920, when the American woman earned the right to vote for the first time. We are making progress as a society when we embrace the idea of gender equality, but one question remains.

How can every woman create the results she wants to see in her life when everything still seems directed by men?

You will discover a simple message in this book: everything is up to you. Women have access to more resources than ever before to build the life that we want.

I appreciate the overall narrative that you will discover in the following pages. It is encouraging, inspirational, and motivating. As women, we can choose to succeed. We can make the choice to allow ourselves to become empowered. If we want to be successful, then we can make our goals become a reality.

You are the *creator* of your dreams. There are more women in formal paid employment today than at any other point in human history. We make up 40% of the global labor force, making positive impacts in our communities every day.

There are numerous examples in the following pages of women who dared to take the first step on their empowerment journey and never look back. By bringing a message of hope to the world, they made a positive global impact because they put in the work to make their own luck.

Now *it* is our turn. Are you ready to become an Impactor?

Hazel Herrington

Introduction

Reading this book, expect to learn why the amazing women featured are referred to as 'The Impactors'.

All the contributors shared their stories of transformation and growth from adversity to achievement, their strategies of how they have managed to overcome their fears and anxiety and their journey towards becoming global impactors.

Chosen to become the Celebrity Coach for these hardworking women on Team Vicky in The Next Impactor competition, the brainchild of Local Entrepreneurs Jeff Levin (Founder of the www.co-opmovement.com) and Loren Michaels Harris (Founder of The Power of We Symposium), I was inspired to put this book together. *The idea behind The Next Impactor is that this world needs hope, inspiration and positive role models driven to positively always influence others.*

It was during our first meeting that I thought of putting together and publishing this book knowing fully well that we are making history and I want this to be documented. This would help us to leave a legacy behind and aid in our philanthropy. The proceeds from the sale of this book will be going to assist a couple of orphanages in Nigeria namely Christ Orphanage Home, Ondo and Finger of God Orphanage Lagos.

My hope is not only that you enjoy reading this book, but I also hope that it is thought-provoking, and you realize, that if the women in this book can become global impactors, you can too. My message to you is that being an impactor is not about being perfect in every way, but about being vulnerable, embracing your vulnerability and then focusing on lifting other people up.

Always remember that being an impactor is never about what you know or say; it is what you do.

Vicky Omifolaji

Contents

Dedication 3
Foreward 4
Introduction 6
Chapter 1: Vicky Omifolaji 9
Chapter 2: Barbara Ellison 17
Chapter 3: Amiee K. Boswinkle 32
Chapter 4: Tiauna Ross 54
Chapter 5: Beth Olson 66
Chapter 6: Antonietta Morrone Birdsell 84
Chapter 7: Noelle Agape 106
Chapter 8: Sharon Ton 124
Chapter 9: Elizabeth Schmidt 137
Chapter 10: Emily Seelman 139
Chapter 11: Sophia Greenstein 142
Chapter 12: Allison Ferrante 144
Conclusion 147
About the Author 153

Chapter 1

VICKY OMIFOLAJI

Vicky Omifolaji is the owner of Vicky Omifolaji Consulting and Counselling Services based in Melbourne Victoria. Popularly known as Coach Vicky, she has dedicated her life to helping people by the hundreds, thousands in fact.

Vicky achieved a double master's degree in counselling and social work respectively and became a licensed/clinical accredited counsellor and psychotherapist, or more specifically, a Clinical Adversity Specialist and a Private Achievement Coach. As a Clinical Adversity Authority, she helps people overcome ANY issues causing stress, anxiety or holding them back. In her capacity as a Private Achievement Coach, she helps them accomplish FAR MORE in their career, business or life, than they ever dreamed possible.

The unbelievable transformations she has helped people achieve, from saving them from certain suicide to go on to achieving true greatness, is commendable.

Inspiring Powerful Leaders all over the world through her messages in Australia, Nigeria and Manila in the Philippines, Vicky is the Absolute Expert in Attaining Success.

She is the Founder & Chief Trainer of the ADVERSITY-TO-ACHIEVEMENT ACADEMY which teaches people to overcome their challenges; conquer their fears; and attain their goals and dreams. She is also the Founder & Director of the Global Achievers Magazine and The GLOBAL ACHIEVERS FOUNDATION (non-profit) – Inspiring and Leading a new generation with the tools, resources, methods, and means to attain their greater potential.

Vicky has authored nine amazing books, with millions of her books sold on different platforms around the world.

She is happily married to Dr Stephen Omifolaji and they have three wonderful children – Shina, Victor and Lola.

It was only a few days ago that I watched a Netflix film a documentary titled The Black Godfather. The documentary is about a man called Clarence Avant, a black American man well respected by everyone due to the impact he made in so many people's lives. His story resonated with me.

Clarence has been described by Newsweek as "one of the most powerful and renowned people within the entertainment industry and yet he may also be the most elusive too." His name is synonymous to success, as further explained by Newsweek. This is because his influence aided so many entertainment celebrities and political leaders who turned to him for counselling and guidance. He has been credited for his role in launching the careers of many while remaining anonymous.

Clarence Avant, The Black Godfather, is the epitome of an Impactor. Yet, he did not kill anyone to get to where he was, to where he is, this paramount position of power and influence. He became The Black Godfather because of his love, his kindness and ultimate respect for others.

Avant's biographical documentary provoked me to reflect on my life and this journey that has ultimately led to me becoming a coach for the global competition *The Next Impactor*. An inspiring characteristic of Mr Avant is that he is a connector. With the help of is networking amongst other things, he serves as the integral bridge between people and the exclusive opportunity whereby one can reach their ultimate potential. This for me, ultimately emphasizes the weight behind my own saying, "My network is my net worth". I deeply believe no one can do life alone. Therefore, in order to make it in the business world, you must spend time developing relationships and expanding your network. I personally have been doing a lot of networking which consequently led me to leave my comfort zone. However, by spreading my wings, my life has been impacted in an extremely positive way and I would not be where I am today without this.

When I was informed that I have been picked to be one of the five coaches for The Next Impactor competition, I gladly said yes knowing I would be provided opportunities to further grow my network. Ten brilliant women were picked to be in my team, and it has been one of my greatest experience yet.

Being chosen by the founders and directors of The Next Impactor competition, Loren Michael Harris and Jeff Levin to be a coach to these amazing women around the world, humbled me and I reflected on how I came to be where I am. I thought about my life's journey thus far; and the comment made by Loren to me when I asked him why he chose me resonated. Loren commented, "Impactors don't see themselves as Impactors, but they make ripples wherever they do. Their life's purpose is to impact other people's lives without making noise about it and that is who you are Vicky."

I was born and raised in Nigeria, where I lived until I was 24. At that age, I got married and moved with my husband to South Africa, where we lived for years.

My dad was a lecturer at a university and my mom was a teacher in a secondary school. I am the first of five children. My father became a pastor in an Anglican Church, eventually rose up in ranks and became an Archdeacon till he retired at the age of 70. I was raised by two parents who I will classify as strict, very, very strict, especially my mother. My father was the one that I'd tend to go to for almost everything, because my mom was extremely strict and especially on me being the first child. So, I got all the discipline and beating. I got all the talking to whenever I had done something wrong. I will share one experience with you about something that happened, that really still is a 'big deal' to me and has stayed with me. It's somehow guided me in all that I do and have done, even to this day.

The story goes:

I would have been around 11 years old, my parents invited one man, a very rich man to come to our church. It was to an event that we had at the church at the time. This man, this rich man was invited to be the chairman of that event. As a chairman, he was expected to donate a significant amount of money to the church. So after the church program, we invited the man and a few people that came with him to a reception, for a meal.

We cooked a lovely meal, set the table really nicely; and the man had his meal. When everyone finished, we packed up the dining table and we cleaned up. I recall serving myself a plate full, from the leftover, then as I was about to sit down to start eating the food, I remember saying to myself, "now I can sit down and relax and have the leftover of a rich man". My mom turned to look at me. I could see the disappointment in her face. She then said, "why would you say something like that? The man is a rich man because he worked hard to be. Why are you happy because you are going to be having the leftover of a rich man? So, what's stopping you from working hard, and being a rich person yourself? What's stopping you? With this mindset, you are going to be a second-class citizen for the rest of your life. You have to change your mindset so that you can always be ahead and not in the bottom."

As she lectured me, I found myself rolling my eyes in my head, and I thought, "this woman would not even let me rest." So, I left the food that I had served myself and I went to my room. Lying on my bed, I started reflecting on what mom said earlier on. Then I thought, 'oh my goodness, it's true. I shouldn't be happy because a rich man had leftovers and I was happy just having that. What's stopping me from being a rich woman myself, what's stopping me from working hard, and being the person that people reckon with? What's stopping me from working hard to be the great person that God has created me to be?"

That was the beginning of changing my life. My mom wouldn't let that moment pass without using it as an opportunity to educate me in LifeSkills. When I look at things, stuff that happened and impacted my life when I was growing up, this is number one, because that has been my guide. That lesson has shaped the way I deal with life. If somebody else had already done it, I can do it too, it's not a 'big deal'. And that's what I do, I push, and I push, and I push always trying to be better, to grow.

When I talk about my struggles, and how I overcame, I'm talking about the many struggles I've had throughout my life. I've been met with challenges and struggles since I was only a child. There was a time as a young kid, I used to struggle with learning. I did not understand things the same way other people did. My style of learning had always been very different. Unfortunately, education systems aren't designed to fit into how different kids learn, and so I struggled.

I had to adapt, alter my way of understanding so as to not fail in my grade. I did everything to not get behind in my studies. I learned to make friends with kids who coped better with the learning style and excelled in my school. I was strategic to not simply choose those who excel but look further and find those who could explain things to me in the way that I could understand. That was what I did all through high school and even through university. I would make friends with people who excelled academically, people who have goals but wouldn't make fun of me, people who could teach me. That was how I managed to learn and excel.

I attended St. Margaret's Anglican grammar school, a public school yet somewhat private school for girls. At school they grouped us in classes based on our grades, so we had "the clever class" and the not so clever ones.

The top class, clever class, was comprised of the learners who placed from first to thirtieth in the grade. Although learning was difficult, I knew I couldn't place beyond the thirtieth place or else I would be in trouble with my parents. They expected me to do well in school. By now, I'm sure you understand that attaining an education was a struggle for me, a huge challenge. To get an understanding of the school material, I would read all night. Something that would take somebody else 20 minutes, would take me hours. Even so, I knew I had to do it, I had to get it done and so I pushed. I kept on doing, and I did. I tried my best. So, my struggle started when I was only a child, but I refused to allow them to define me. I finished school, completed university successfully and I got married.

The Journey of becoming a celebrity coach for The Next Impactor competition hasn't been an easy one. Through Private Mental Health Clinic which I started in 2012, I work with clients who struggle in life due to lack of life skills. I came up with the idea of running group sessions for young people once a week, providing participants with skills that include anger management, goal planning, emotional self-awareness, anxiety management, communication skills, relationship skills, and problem-solving skills. Gippsland LifeSkills Program Incorporated became a registered charity organisation with the Australian Charity Organisation.

The implementation of my idea saw so many young people benefitting from attending the programs. Referrals started pouring in from schools. I felt so proud to be the founder of an impactful program for young people in my community. I felt encouraged to push, to do more.

I later set up programs for parents and isolated people in the community called Coffee n Company. Many people volunteer to help out with facilitating, fundraising and marketing the programs.

The success of my not for profit organisations triggered my thirst for doing more within my community, my country of birth and the global world. For me, it wasn't about making tons of money but about making changes in other people's lives positively.

Reflecting on my growth, my achievements, giving back and helping to build my community, I can fully understand why I was chosen to be a coach. Being an impactor is about being genuine in what you do for others. There is no space for fakery. Be true to yourself and others.

Chapter 2

BARBARA ELLISON

BIO:

Barbara Ellison is the Founder of Timed Partner Media located in Cortland, IL. She is quick to mention that she didn't see the value in becoming an SEO Expert (Search Engine Optimization). She literally walked away from the training opportunity. But, Fate has a way of making its path known. The very next day she realized that learning SEO would help her own coaching business. It would also give her the opportunity to help others who were in the same boat that she was which was building a new business and not knowing how to get ranked on the Search Engines.

Her mission is to help businesses be **Well Known** & **Well paid** for what they bring to the marketplace. With that mission in mind she became a member of the **Co-Opvertising Network.** Barbara joined the Co-Op as a new approach to marketing her business. The Co-Op approach of helping others first aligned with her own values of how she wanted to do her business. It has become so much more.

Through the Co-Op she learned that there is an alarming number of children who only eat when they are at school. Barbara has embraced the goal of the Co-Op to cover the local food bank's budget for peanut butter.

Barbara is the mother to two grown sons Andrew and Malcolm. Her husband David passed away in 2011. In 2012 she moved out of her home and rented it to her former daughter-in-law. In 2014 she moved back into her house with the new family. Countless pets and always extra pets. Two of the grandchildren work at the local pet shelter. It can be chaotic and noisy but what a blessing it has been!

It is a bustling home west of Chicago, IL. There are three adults and 10 children who all call her Grammy. There are five biological grandchildren and five acquired. Some through marriage, some through adoption or through guardianship.

Born and raised in Montreal, Canada, Barbara moved to the United States when she married at age 21. Being divorced she has maintained a cordial relationship because of the grandchildren.

Barbara loves to crochet and makes baby blankets for the We Care Pregnancy Center in DeKalb, IL. She is an avid reader. She is active in her church and loves Praise and Worship Music.

What is exciting her this summer? She is taking singing lessons. Singing in a band is on her bucket list of things she wants to do. Also on her list: walk the Great Wall of China, visit the Australian Outback, safari in Kenya and host a business retreat in Bali.

Barbara Ellison

Certified & Licensed BankCode Trainer

815-748-4676

Questions asked... and answered..

As I sat down to write this chapter, I was looking over the questions that Coach Vicky gave us as a guideline. I was struck by the questions and doubts going through my mind, such as, "can I really be a part of a book?" and, "what do I have to contribute?" I was praying about where to start and the Lord spoke to my heart and said to just start - that the words would come.

I have to say that I never thought that I would ever be a part of such an incredible group of ladies as I have found with Team Vicky. To start, entering a competition like The Next Impactor was not something that I even dreamed of doing. How can I describe the feelings that have surfaced and the growth that has happened to me since the beginning of this impactor journey?

A happy childhood...

A good place to start my story is with my childhood. I realize now that I lived a pretty nice childhood. I had loving parents and sisters, and while we fought like cats and dogs, much like every other family that I know of, we were close and supportive. I learned the lessons of routine and structure early from my Mom. Sunday was church, Monday was laundry, Tuesday was ironing etc. We lived a planned life, except during the summer when it was a free for all. My dad would come home from work always right around 5:00 pm. My mom would have everything ready for a picnic and we would head to Crystal Beach. Our picnics were not like other people's picnics or like the picnics that I have now. We had plates with knives and forks and a tablecloth for the table. There was a vase with fresh flowers, and we all sat at the same table and had conversation about what we had done that day. We had summer programs at the park every day to talk about. My dad would also tell us about airplanes at the airport and what made them all different. As I am writing this, I have a smile on my face because those were such great times. Did these fond memories shape me into the woman that I am today? Absolutely! Were there terrible memories also? Absolutely, but I choose not to dwell on those. I have realized through hearing the stories of these wonderfully warm, gifted and powerful ladies of Team Vicky, my childhood was privileged in comparison to some. I am truly grateful to each and every one of them for sharing with me the traumas and the tragedies that impacted their lives, as it has helped me to be more empathetic and grateful.

Gratitude

I was talking to my sister, Elizabeth, in Canada on the phone as I was out walking my dog, Daisy. It was a beautiful day and I was so happy to be able to talk to her. I was telling her about how excited I am about this competition. I was struck by how amazing it was that I can walk my dog, talk on the phone to someone who is 1000 miles away and think nothing of it, as I sat down to write about it on my iPad. We live in an awesome world of technology. I have been listening to several investment celebs who are predicting radical changes in the tech world that will revolutionize our world even more. It is exciting to think about what we will be able to accomplish as Impactors and yet sometimes it is also an overwhelming and scary thought as well.

A change of perspective...

I was telling Elizabeth about the memories I am sharing here about our upbringing and we laughed about some of the memories that we had. One of our funny recollections was that on her wedding day, my uncle Albert, who was an outgoing entrepreneur, pulled up in front of our house in his brand-new gold Cadillac convertible. My Mom about croaked!! I always thought that she was embarrassed about it because it was so flashy. It was showing off his wealth to the neighbors and she was so conservative. The funny thing about it now, as I listened to Elizabeth's memory of that same day, I realized that Mom was upset because this was her daughter's wedding day and her brother took all the attention away from that fact. WOW! What a revelation for me. I can always remember Mom saying to me that I was so much like uncle Albert, and I remember feeling that that was not necessarily a good thing as my mom didn't seem to value the priorities and activities of my uncle. The next day we were sitting at the restaurant and I remember trying to be quieter, smaller and less me as it felt that being my "ON" self at the wedding the previous day had not been well received. My aunt looked at my mom and asked her what was wrong with me? My Mom immediately turned to me and asked what was wrong with me? In that moment, as a 16-year-old, I thought that there was no way to win. If I was my outgoing self, that was wrong, and if I was quiet, that was also wrong. I spent the rest of my life trying to mold myself into whatever I thought would please everyone else. Thank goodness for personal development seminars, courses and coaches that have helped me set boundaries and find my self-worth. One day, as I was telling my coach this part of my life and how I felt "stuck" because of it, he looked at me and gave me the best piece of advice; "Barbara", he said, "Reframe that Story!!". That got my attention. Were there positives about being like Uncle Albert? Of course there were! He was ambitious, brave, outgoing, passionate and self-confident. I am now building a successful business with a mission to change the world BECAUSE I AM LIKE MY UNCLE ALBERT. DUH!!!!! All these years I had been fighting this and now I embrace it. It is amazing. My piece of advice to others is this; if you have something in your past that is holding you back and keeping you stuck, confront it, reframe it, get over it and move on. I know that I am a better person for having experienced this and I am the person I am today partly because of it.

A Defining Moment...

I think that one of the most defining moments of my life was when my husband David passed away in October 2011. I expected for David and I to grow old together, and to dance at our great grandchildren's weddings. At 60, I became a widow and realized that I had never truly been on my own before, and I was now totally responsible for every one of my decisions. The good ones, and the not so good ones. Remember me saying that I lived a life of structure growing up? Well, David was also a person of structure - he liked to have a plan for everything. I could change his plans; however, he wasn't always very happy about it. You can imagine what it was like for me to now have to totally rely on myself for structure and planning. Can I tell you right off the bat that I didn't do so well! For the first 2 years, I just floated along, going to work (working in the restaurant business was a Godsend because I had people contact) and yet I don't really remember those years. I was in such a fog that they are just a blur of grief and loneliness.

My Journey to faith...

I want to share a bit of our history together. David and I got married in 1996 and we had a lovely home out in the country. One day I was checking the weather channel for possible tornadoes in our area and I have to tell you, I was not used to being aware of tornadoes. I grew up in Montreal, Canada where we had severe storms but never tornadoes. I would panic every time one of the sirens would go off (we lived 3 blocks from the siren so it was loud).

As I was waiting for the weather report, an infomercial came on. The lady asked, "do you feel like you have it all and yet know that there is something missing in your life?" That question stopped me in my tracks and brought me to tears. I had a wonderful husband who adored me. Children who loved me. A beautiful home in the quiet suburbs. A business that David and I were building together was gaining traction. How could I have those "things" and yet feel that there was something "missing". I watched the entire infomercial and went out and bought the book. The author was Gwen Shamblin creator of the Weigh Down Workshop. I enrolled in her program that was being sponsored by one of the local churches. That program turned my life upside down, although now I think of it as being right side up.

Growing up, we went to church every Sunday. I attended Sunday school. I went through CGIT (Canadian Girls in Training) and youth groups. I knew the facts about Jesus. I did not learn how to be in a relationship with him on a daily basis. To let Him guide me and Love me. I started the program in October and on Jan 1, 1998, I knew I needed more. The journey began.

I thought I could be a "stay at home Christian". I watched the Hour of Power with Robert Schuler, Joyce Meyers, Creflo Dollar and I listened to Christian music on K-Love Radio. That did work for a while as it got me back into the way of prayer and seeking direction for areas of my life. (David thought I was brainwashed and he would have nothing to do with any of it.)

Then March of 1998 came. I was being all spiritual and praying about what I should do to grow as a Christian. It was like an audible voice in my head saying, "GO TO CHURCH". One of my business associates had asked me to come to church on many occasions. Whenever we got together to talk about her business, she mentioned going to church with her. (imagine that). I called her and told her my story of hearing the "voice of God" telling me to go to church. Her first words were "Praise the Lord" and she gave me the details about where to go.

Sunday morning rolls around and off I go to Glad Tidings Assembly of God church in DeKalb, IL. As I walked in, it didn't seem any different than the church that I had grown up in. Then the worship service started with a band and singers. I grew up with only an organ playing hymns. This band was singing praise and worship songs like the ones I had been listening to on K-Love. They were phenomenal. After the first song, I turned to Phyllis and said, "this is a Pentecostal church isn't it?" She said yes and asked why?

I told her the story of when I was eight years old. We went to a Christmas Cantata at my cousin's church which was a Pentecostal church. I didn't know what that meant, all I knew was that we were going to a Christmas concert that my cousin was taking part in. During the concert, it is the practice in their church to do an altar call. People have the opportunity to receive Jesus into their lives. I started to get up and go forward. My mom grabbed my arm and told me to sit down. I turned to her and told her that they were "calling" me to go up to the front. She was insistent that I sit down. "But Mom, they are calling me!!" It was so powerful a feeling but at 8 years old I had no reference point to explain it. When my Mom insisted again that I sit down saying "we don't do things like that in our church." I sat down. Over the years I thought about it once in a while. Phyllis looked at me and all she said was "Wow and Praise the Lord".

What got my attention in that service was when the worship leader Sherry stopped in the middle of the next song and said, "we have to sing Amazing Grace!" She started to sing before the rest of the worship team could even get their music out. It was not a hymn that they were planning to sing that day.

Amazing Grace has always been one of my favorite hymns and in that moment, I knew beyond any doubt that God loved ME!!! The Me: flawed, scarred and weak. I **knew** that He had sent His son Jesus to die for me! It was in that moment that I was washed clean of everything that I had ever done, and I was Forgiven!!! Amazing Grace, the hymn, became amazing grace for real in my life.

That day I was forever changed, and David saw the difference. I filled our home with praise and worship music. He came from a family who had never attended church except for weddings and funerals. He didn't know what to do with all the "Christian" stuff that I was now immersing myself in. He only made one comment and it was about the music. Being a musician himself, he said that it wasn't like any church music he had ever heard. For 2 years I asked him to come to church with me and he resisted every week.

I asked him to learn Amazing Grace and then I would ask him to play it for me. I would then pray that the words of that hymn would become real to him too. And then one day they did! I came home from work and he was practicing a Ray Bolz song called the Anchor Holds. When I asked him about it, all he said was that he "had to" learn it and I knew that his journey had begun. David went on to become a worship leader at our church. He was a deacon and then an elder. Until his passing, he never lost his faith even in the midst of the cancer that was so painful and debilitating.

It was the most horrific time of my life. To watch this vibrant man, the love of my life become a shrivelled shell, yet I wouldn't trade the years we had together.

My new life...

I still remember the day I woke up from my grief. It was October 13, 2013 and realized David had died - not me, and I wondered what was I going to do with the rest of my life?

The lesson that I want to share for this period of my life is this; mourn for as long as you need to, but then pick yourself up and know that not only can you survive the loss (whether it's a marriage, a career, a spouse, a business) but that you can also go on to bigger and better things. Things that will excite you, challenge you and take you so far out of your comfort zone that it is exhilarating.

My journey into entrepreneurship had started long before this period though. I understood the concept of building your own business from an early age and recognized all the benefits and the freedom. When David and I had gotten married, he joined me in the business that I was already involved in and it was something that we did together. I had dabbled with network marketing for years and had been fairly successful. When I lost him, I lost the business too because I just couldn't go back to it without him. I needed to discover what I wanted to do now, I knew what I didn't want, but had no clue what I did want or how to get it.

I needed change!!!! Over the next 5 years, I experimented with all sorts of things, I started with online marketing, switched to affiliate marketing, switched to coaching (which I still love to do, as my purpose is to serve God, learn and then to teach what I learn) then switched back to network marketing, and that was a total disaster not only did I make some really naive decisions, I fell prey to not seeking advice and then felt that I had lost everything: money, confidence and my excellent credit score. I have always been so trusting and was always the one who wanted to help others So, now here I am in recovery from a loss again!!! What am I going to do now? I made the decision to get training that would benefit me across multiple areas, so I took a course in how to do search engine optimization. Even though it is so different from anything that I have ever done, I am totally enjoying it. I feel a renewed sense of purpose in helping others because I feel that if I can help others have a successful business, they would be able to provide for their family and then be able to give back to the world around them.

Soon after, I faced the daunting task of building a business, and connecting with people with similar goals and interests. Did I know how to do that? NO!!! I made so many mistakes starting out, that I shudder to think about them. What finally turned me around was joining the Co-Opvertising network founded by Jeff Levin, and his wife Lisa. I finally found a group of people who thought the way that I did. The way to be super successful was to help others become successful. One of my favorite quotes is from Zig Ziglar when he says, "you will get everything that you want if you help enough people get what they want!"

I had so many bits and pieces of how to do a business in my repertoire - I was a course junkie, knew lots of what to do, but not how to pull it all together - I had shiny object syndrome to the nth degree - the "let's see what else I can do" distraction, and consequently, I had spent thousands of dollars with not much to show for it. Something had to change!! The Co-op has been the best thing for me - joining it has given me opportunities to share my gifts and expertise, as well as, given me the confidence to join The Next Impactor, a creation of Jeff Levin and Loren Harris.

A new direction...

For the last 40 years, I have been in the restaurant business, from being a bartender to being the floor manager in a fine dining restaurant. How does search engine optimization, building a business and joining the co-op correlate to that? How can I pull all my experience and training together into a cohesive brand that I can market and make a difference? I finally realized my passion, and how I can make it happen. Restaurants need traffic, just like other businesses, so I am now looking into services that will help restaurants be more successful. Jeff is a master at getting to the root of any roadblock, and one day, he asked me what my work history had been. He asked me why I wasn't working with restaurants, when I had 40 years of experience and insight into this market. It was a light bulb moment for me, and when he mentioned the words Restaurant Consultant, it just resonated with me and I knew this is where my talent and experience are best used.

The Next Impactor….

When I mentioned doing things that will get you so far out of your comfort zone that it will be exhilarating (read: scary) - that is where The Next Impactor comes in. Jeff had been saying for quite a while that we needed to "level up" our game and make a difference in the world. My co-op friend and fellow Peanut Butter Challenge Queen, Sharon Ton, said, "oh, for heaven sake Barbara just join the competition!"

I didn't realize what an impact this competition would have on me, and my life until I was chosen to be in the top 50. Even then, I didn't completely grasp how much it would change me, grow me, challenge me and ultimately scare me to death. One of my teammates, Noelle Agape, asked us if we were ready - ready for the next challenge, ready for the exposure, ready for even more personal growth, ready to be The Next Impactor.

To be completely honest, the next day I didn't want to get out of bed - I just wanted to hide in my room and stay under the covers where it felt safe and comfortable. You see, the final challenge was to make a flyer asking people to vote for me. "Isn't that bragging?", I worried. I feared I would look self-absorbed or totally self-serving. My mind was trying to talk me out of going for it and possibly going on to the next phase of elimination down to the top 25 because of fear. It was a Sunday (God has a sense of humor and excellent timing). As I was telling a friend about how I was feeling, I broke down and said, with the quiet conviction that only God can give, that the answer to my dilemma would be found at church. Off to church I went, and the answer was there.

One of the messages that morning at church was that we all have a purpose and that God will give us EVERYTHING we need to accomplish it. As I listened, I knew beyond any doubt that this competition was bigger than me and my fear of the unknown. This competition was about being an Impactor, someone who is willing to step up and make a difference in the world. Wasn't that what I had been looking for my whole life?

In that moment, my purpose and my passion crystallized. For years, I have had a dream running around in my head that I wanted to create "Family Adventure Farms". A safe place where at-risk kids and their families could come to learn new skills that they could use to earn an income, as well as developing other skills or trades that would excite them, build confidence, mend relationships, help them to realize that their individual successes, and just have fun going on outdoor adventures. This dream is now so big and so real that when Noelle asked us what scares us - this is it for me. This vision is greater than me. I am not only an Impactor; I am a million-dollar philanthropist. My dream to have "Adventure Farms" all over the world will take millions of dollars, millions of people and millions of resources, and I will be the one to see it come to life.

Doing one thing differently...

Another question was, "if there was one thing that I could do differently what would it be? I would take the plunge right away with the Co-Op and hire Jeff to get my business together. I spent almost 7 months trying to do it on my own and of course, didn't make any headway. I had so many roadblocks. I've already talked about some of the serious setbacks that have occurred. I didn't mention that the company I was working with got shut down by the FTC. I know that all those things, those challenges are part of being successful. I always think of the saying that you can't have a testimony if you never have a test. How can you relate to what others are going through if you haven't gone through anything yourself?

I am an entrepreneur who wants to make a difference in the world. Yet, over the years I have doubted that, changed my mind about it, tried to ignore it, and wondered what to do with that.

Before I married David, I was married to my first husband for 20 years. It ended in divorce, which was devastating for my sons. At the time, I had a job that moved me around fairly often, so the boys opted to live with their Dad so as not to change schools. I never once thought that I would be divorced but I had to pick myself up and go on. I look back now and I have wondered what I could have done differently to preserve the family unit.

What leads to the breakup of a family? I think that one reason is that we are not taught relationship skills. How to talk to each other. As a Personality Science Trainer, I now know that quite often the very things that attracted us to our partners become the very thing that drives us apart. We are also not taught personal development skills. Things like how to be fulfilled in our career, how to be physically fit, how to be spiritually healthy and the list goes on.

This is part of the vision that I have for my Adventure Farms. It started out that it would be about creating a safe place for at-risk families to come and learn communication skills. Maybe learn some practical skills that they could use to earn income or get out of debt or so many other issues that families face.

Since being in the Next Impactor Competition, my vision has expanded even more globally. What if we could have companies, politicians, heads of states, etc. have a place to come to, learn communication, teamwork and strive for world peace? It would be AWESOME!!!

Barbara Ellison

Certified & Licensed BankCode Trainer

815-748-4676

Chapter 3

Amiee K. Boswinkle

Biography for Amiee K. Boswinkle

Amiee K. Boswinkle is a visionary, a creator of beauty and a highly gifted intuitive.

Amiee found her way out of the darkness and into the light when debilitating trauma, PTSD and addictions took over her life and she couldn't find reprieve from conventional health care or therapies. For years, she suffered from the shame of childhood sexual assault which led her down the path of alcoholism, drug addiction and binge eating disorder. One day she woke up facing the possibility of spending a year in jail after she received her third DUI, so she decided something really had to change. She took matters into her own hands and studied the human body until was able to heal herself through nutrition and alternative therapies and treatments, when all hope seemed lost.

Today, Amiee touches the hearts and lives of people suffering from trauma, PTSD and addictions helping them break free from the prison of their own minds through 1:1s and group work with clients and sharing her story of experience, strength and hope through public speaking and workshops. Amiee is the PROUD owner of her business - Connections Restored.

She holds a B.A. in Psychology from Ball State University, is a Certified RMT and is a Certified Health Coach. Amiee is currently part of the Top 50 Contestants on Season One of The Next Impactor Competition.

Amiee has had the opportunity to speak on platforms such as the Global Health Summit, Creating Infinite Health, and has spoken three times on the Facebook Summit, Beyond the Limits, she has been a public speaker for both Unity of Northwest Indiana, Unity in the Dunes, One Best Life, Tinker's Attic and St. Catherine Hospital's Breaking the Stigma of Mental Health Event. Amiee has been featured as the guest blogger for My Lilianas and she has also been featured on The Corrie Lo Show

Podcast, speaking on The Role of Nutrition in Addictions. Amiee desires to publicly share her story of experience, strength and hope through public speaking around the world. She is one of the contributing authors in the book "Victorious Women Overcoming Mediocrity". Her story is titled, "Darkness, Darkness Everywhere."

Amiee desires to heal the wounds of the weary and lost, through her teachings; and desires to uplift the vibrational energy of humanity with the wisdom she's acquired through the lessons of her lifetime.

Amiee's philosophy embodies:

"Fear has created separateness in our world. The connection we are seeking is love. Infuse the world with you, your truth, your essence and ignite the fire necessary for change. Love will change the nation. The nation starts within you." - Amiee K. Boswinkle

"Incandescent"

I look back at life and wonder how I'm even the same person.

A few weeks ago, I was being introduced as a guest speaker at a Mental Health event; where the other speakers and I were relaying to the audience of a little over 100 people, on how to break the stigma surrounding this topic that is needed to be talked about more. I stood there listening to her read my bio and my head went blank. I thought, who is this person she is introducing. This momentary glitch in my consciousness made the moment feel so surreal. I knew she was reading the words I had written, but in that moment, I had a hard time connecting to that version of me.

I walked up to the microphone to make a small joke- "Who is THAT person you just announced?" The audience half chuckled, not knowing I was half joking and half in shock.

I took a deep breath and proceeded with, in my opinion and based on the way the audience reaction, my best speech to date; on how to deal with the physiological stressors of stress response in the CNS (Central Nervous System) and brain and calm down the fight or flight response in the body that will allow the adrenal glands to produce less cortisol. In my opinion, Endocrine System responses are not talked about enough and are huge precursors to disease: and getting any, and all information out into the world is certainly VERY important to me.

I wish I had been taught the things I teach now when I was in school, maybe life would have been different for me. Maybe it wouldn't. Either way, I'm teaching it now because of the deep importance this and many other health related issues are felt deeply in my heart to share with the world.

I come back to this moment, right now. At this current moment, friends, I'm sitting in shock (again) at being in the Top 50 contestants in a competition called The Next Impactor. How I arrived here was a long and winding path full of plot twists and near-death experiences. As I stated above, I used to be a completely different person. I'm a little bit in shock over this as well.

Overcoming great pain and hardship is a true demonstration of what the human experience is all about in my eyes. To watch people transform pain to power is an ultimate truth. If we all dig deep down inside to our drive - the part of us that tells us to keep moving forward, we can move mountains. We all have this. We can all move mountains, it's just a matter of deciding which direction to move the mountain. In my life, I know some of the choices I made moved the mountain right on top of me and I carried the weight of the world on my shoulders. Some of the choices I made moved the mountain far away from me and I was able to breathe again and see with ultimate clarity. I gained a freedom I had never experienced in my life before. The ultimate experience of life is the fact that we get to make choices. Every day, in every way, we make choices. Some choices are empowering, others are disempowering. What I've learned to do is make wise choices. Choices that empower me and move me towards the things I desire to have more of in life. I didn't always understand I had a choice. Looking back on my life now, I can truthfully say I know I had a choice in every decision I made. Waking up to that consciously was a journey for me. I still practice self-mastery in this area. I will for the remainder of my life. I'm grateful I've become aware of this.

Life wasn't always like this for me. For the first 40 years of my life, life was mechanical. Life was painful. Life was full of traumatic experiences that created PTSD and addictions for me. I didn't realize the prison cell I had created around my own mind. My thoughts, beliefs and habits dictated a world of pain. The choices I made, kept me stuck. I lived in a hamster wheel of shame, guilt, blame, judgment and denial. Healing these low vibrational states was a journey, as is all of life. I'm grateful to have woken up to the power of this new awareness and empowered choice that can be made from it.

To understand this fully, I must take you back on a journey in time with me, so you can see, friends, one of the many hoops I jumped through and the wonder of how I overcame such darkness.

I have always been shy, introverted and intuitive. I always trusted my gifts, my knowing, it was just such an innate part of me. What I didn't trust was the way I thought the world perceived me.

I was so painfully shy that in first grade my teacher thought I had special needs because I couldn't talk. This was common for me. I could do anything you asked, but I could never find my voice. I believe this was because of the sexual abuse I had endured at a very young age, where I was told to never tell, or I wouldn't be loved anymore. So, I didn't tell for many years of my life and I shut down and lost my voice.

I never felt like I fit in. The teachers in the special need's classroom saw that I didn't belong there and sent me back to the regular classroom and I just existed. I didn't connect. My teacher was kind but didn't work with me. I was put in all the low-level learning circles. I created stories in my head of how I was stupid, fat and ugly because of this. I remained separate, isolated and alone in my mind. Even when I was playing with what friends I did make, I always felt all alone. There was no connection because I didn't know how to let people in.

This belief system followed me through high school and into college.

In college I was able to connect with friends that I felt close to. By this time though, I was becoming a full-fledged alcoholic. I became an alcoholic the first time I drank beer. I had had a few wine coolers before this, but never anything more. I remember drinking my first sip of beer and by the time the 32 oz red Solo plastic cup was half empty, I was out of my mind drunk. I kept drinking. I blacked out. I was at a party with people I hadn't known all that long and woke up on a pile of coats.

You would think this would have scared me, but I wanted more. This was the first time in my life I ever felt free. No inhibitions, no chains, nothing holding me back, free. I couldn't wait for the next party so I could drink more, and more parties there were.

It was an interesting balance of going to school full time, working full time and partying full time. It took me 3 semesters to perfect my schedule. Once I did, it was game on. I wore my partying abilities like a badge of honor. I called myself a functional alcoholic, which I deemed as ok because I was still able to pay bills, go to work, go to school, turn in homework assignments and maintain relatively good grades.

There was a demon inside me though. She only emerged when I drank to the point of blackout and to me the only way TO drink was to the point of blackout. I was happiest in this place. I was free. Free to say the things I wanted to say. I thought I had control. I thought I was kind and loving. I was free to wear the things I wanted to wear. I could go anywhere, do anything and be exactly who I wanted to be. Of course, this image was skewed. Drunk Amiee believed she was the same as Sober Amiee. This was the farthest thing from the truth. I was my very own version of Dr. Jekyll and Mr. Hyde.

Sober Amiee was shy. She was quiet and soft-spoken. She was intelligent and fun to be with. She liked adventure and creativity. This version of Amiee lived in a lot of fear, shame and guilt as well. She knew when she woke up the next morning that she had created a lot of havoc in her blackout states of drinking. You would think that I would have stopped drinking, but I only wanted more. It was an escape to me. When I was drunk, I was free. Free in a way I didn't know how to be when I was sober. By creating an alternate reality through the use of alcohol and drugs, I didn't have to deal with the real problems going on in my life.

What were those problems? Feeling alone, Isolated. I lived in utter self-hatred and shame. I told myself frequently nobody liked me, that I was stupid, fat and ugly. I told myself that I didn't deserve to live.

Drugs. Yes. This is a big part of my story too. Drugs amplified the effects of my blackout. I was always chasing a higher high or a lower low. I took any and all drugs, I wasn't picky. I wasn't a huge fan of "uppers" but, like I said, I wasn't picky.

In time, my thoughts, feelings and emotions amplified with the intensity of my drug and alcohol use. What was created were suicidal tendencies which led down the road to suicide attempts.

I maintained my composure and graduated from college with a B.A. in Psychology from Ball State University located in Muncie, Indiana in the United States. Where I lacked composure was with my friendships and with my boyfriend at that time. I can't tell you how many interventions they tried to do with me. How many heart-to-heart conversations they had with me when I was sober enough to hear them properly. They were afraid for my life. They were tired of the person I became when I used. They were at the end of their patience with me.

My black hole expanded farther and deeper. I lived to drink and use drugs. All I wanted to do was go into my alternate reality every time I could. It was here, I didn't have to deal with the problems of my life. It was here I felt safe. Reality felt scary. I had to talk to people. I had to look them in the eye. I had to try and manage conversations with them. I had to be a contributing member to society, pay my dues. In my alternate reality I could be free. Free, free, free. Free to say what I wanted to say. Most of the things I said in this space were vile and mean. I was in a lot of inner pain and I was miserable. I wanted people to live there with me. I wanted people to really understand and stand there with me. Luckily, the people in my life were really, smart and they fought back. They walked away. They wouldn't call. They wouldn't come home. All so they didn't have to feed into my negativity and pain. I honor how intelligent they really were. Understanding that the way people act is only telling you what they truly want is a gift most take a lifetime understanding. I understand this concept now, but I didn't then.

The man I was dating in college, couldn't handle me any longer. He had had enough. Looking back, I see how hard he tried to make it work. I hit his limit. I didn't handle it well, I asked him to hang on. He loved me, he did. He loved the sober, sweet version of me that loved adventure. The version of me that was quiet and sweet and kind. She rarely stayed any length of time though. He hung on as long as he could. I asked him to keep dating me until a certain date, telling him on this date I was going to move back home to Griffith, IN. He agreed out of kindness. Looking back, I see the honor and love in his choice.

I was lost in the darkest of holes. Broken and ashamed. I broke down. I started taking even more drugs and alcohol. I had a high tolerance at this point. The amount of multiple substances I could put into my body was alarming. Most people would have overdosed and possibly died from the amounts my body could handle. I was breaking down. My thoughts, feelings and emotions were screaming at me to die. So, I began to slowly make claims of wanting to die which led to being totally blacked out and attempting suicide. I'm not exactly sure how many times I've been in and out of psychiatric wards for suicide attempts. It's many. It's a wonder I'm still alive. It's only by the grace of my higher power, which I choose to call The Universe, that I'm still here.

I started to attempt suicide so much, my friends no longer wanted to be responsible for me, so they called my parents to come and get me to get more help from home. I left Muncie, IN for the first time in 7 years. I was young, but I left the one place where I could feel free and have freedom to return home and try to recover. By this point in my life I had little want for much of anything. What I mean by this is I had very little attachment to physical things like clothes, food, a car, shoes. Most things people need to survive.

When I was 20 and in college, I was renting a home with some friends. One night I woke up to my entire bedroom on fire. I lost everything I owned except my life. I never really recovered from that. It was then I vowed I would never write again (I had been an avid journal writer up until that point) and I would never allow anyone to take pictures of me again. For the most part, that stuck. I wrote papers for school and did do some journaling here and there, but not like I once did. I allowed pictures of me for special occasions. For 20 years I lived my life that way. I lived this way until I started my own business and writing, and pictures became staples that kept my business thriving.

The point to this is, I learned to live with nothing. Then, when I moved back in with my parents because of my unstable mental and emotional health, I took the bare essentials and put the rest in storage in Muncie, IN in a friend's garage at his place of business. I never returned to pick up those items. I learned to live with the bare minimum. I learned that things were things and that many things weren't necessary. I got clothes from friends who didn't want to do the work of pricing them for garage sales or taking them to donation centers.

I got stable enough to find a job at home. However, the drinking and drugging didn't become stable. If anything, it got worse. I found friends to hang out with and my pattern continued. I was a horrible drunk and a kind and loving sober person. My turnaround on friends by this point hit an all-time high. I was getting older and my friends were getting younger because some of them were outgrowing those tendencies and getting married and starting families.

I got my first DUI in August of 2001. I got it on the day of my great-grandmother's funeral. I was pulled over, and while being handcuffed to be taken to jail, I became suicidal. I ended up in the psychiatric ward and missed my great-grandmother's funeral. There was great remorse over this, emotionally and mentally. There was so much shame and guilt. There was so much, what does my family think of me. Where does my family think I am? My parents knew where I was, but I wasn't sure what they told everyone as to my whereabouts. I was so focused on what everyone thought about me that I did the only thing I knew how to do when I got out of the psychiatric ward and that was to drink.

I was introduced to AA (Alcoholic's Anonymous) around this point in time. I had a hard time adjusting here. There were good people there, there were not so good people too. There was me. I played the blame game. I judged my problems as worse as everyone else's. I blamed the men who were trying to ask me out on dates as bad people because I was told the first year in AA that the women stuck with the women and the men stuck with the men. I hated the group sharing. I couldn't stand to have people look at me. By this point, all I saw was the ugly in me. My self-hatred at its worst point. I compared myself right out of the room. If I'm being honest with all of you, I never even put myself in the room.

My first DUI came with the penalty of community service, meeting with a probation officer once a month to check in, fines and losing my driver's license for 6 months.

I think I had my driver's license back just a few weeks before I received my second DUI, February of 2002. Instead of going to jail, I, again, ended up in the psychiatric ward for attempted suicide. I was released. I hired a different lawyer for this offence and received probation, fines, community service and losing my driver's license for one year.

I found myself back in the rooms of AA. I was trying harder this time. I still found it hard to fit in, but I did the things they told me. I found a sponsor, I worked the steps, I had a home meeting, I went to meeting three or more times a week, I stuck with the women, I went to AA supported outings and events when they were offered. It was hard, but I did it. I was scared. I didn't want to get another DUI. I really found myself wanting to not drink. For the first time in many years, I maintained about nine months of continuous sobriety.

Right around the nine months mark was the first time I had a dream that Jesus laid his hands on my head and a golden ball of light that was warm and loving in a way that I had never felt before, was felt in my entire body. The dream was so real. In the dream, Jesus told me to keep helping people. I really took that to heart. I honestly didn't know what he meant, but I will never forget the dream and the way I felt. I fell off track with sobriety not long after this.

I was a good secret keeper. So, I didn't tell anyone and kept attending meetings and I was too ashamed to tell anyone I had fallen off track. So, I lied. I lied about my sobriety so people would think I was a good person. It's funny the things we tell ourselves so we can avoid doing the real work in our lives. What I mean by this is taking a good hard look at ourselves and being honest with ourselves about the damage we create in our own lives. I was lost. I was broken. I was sad. I was still suicidal. I still didn't connect with others and more importantly, I didn't connect with my own self. I lived a life of lies during this time in my life. I hid the parts of me I believed people would judge. I didn't want others to have bad opinions of me. I hid the darkest parts in my very numb heart.

It was during this time of my life that I went from having friends who thought healthy thoughts, who were doing the best they could to live a happy and fulfilling life sober, to having friends who drank and used drugs. In time, I ran across the emotionally and mentally darkest of friends and if I thought life couldn't get any darker, it did.

I met him at a party. Someone I said I dated, but really, we just started using drugs together. I ended up at a party with a friend who had friends I had never met before. I drank to the point of blacking out, then passing out and I was put on top of everyone's coats in a bedroom, out of the way. When I came to, everything in my purse had been stolen, except my car keys, thank goodness! My money was gone, my benzodiazepine prescriptions were gone, my credit cards and I.D.'s were gone. Everything gone, except the purse and my car keys. Of course, when I asked no one knew where they went. I went home with nothing. I filed a police report with that town's police station because I wanted my benzodiazepine prescription refilled.

Now, here's how crazy I had become. At that time in my life I was working for a company that provided supervised visitation between children and their parents who were experiencing difficulties being good parents for various reasons. I worked inside of my county's Government Center Annex building. Surrounded by the prosecutor's office and police officers and very official people. When I went to the police station in the town where I had been at the party where most of my possession's I had on me at the time were stolen, the police officer who took down my report was someone I knew from my job. He asked where I had been, who I was with and what happened. You could tell he was in disbelief around the location I gave him of the party. He looked me dead on in the eye and said something to the effect of – "Amiee, do not ever go to that house again. Do not hang out with those people, they are not good people. I mean it, do not go there ever again."

So, I went there again. Not in defiance, but because I wanted to get high and I needed a place to go with people who would let me do that. I ran into someone knew and started hanging out with him and his friends. I got asked if I wanted to try "Angel Dust." I didn't ask what that was, just said yes and went into the most dream like state I had ever been in. I fell in love with the first snort. The next day I woke up and fainted every time I tried to stand and walk. I had no idea what drug I had been given. I had never had this hard of a time recovering from a hangover before. I wanted to sleep but couldn't.

It was Thanksgiving. I was supposed to be at my parents. I called them and said I would be late. I crawled to the bathroom of the house where I was and tried to stand and couldn't. I felt sick to my stomach. I was cold and clammy. I eventually found my way to my car and drove home. I walked in the house, told my parents I was sick and went and laid down in their room and went to sleep for hours. When I woke up, I left without visiting my parents and went straight back to the house I was at earlier.

When I arrived, the "Angel Dust" guy was there. I asked him what he gave me. He said it was heroin. I asked for more and didn't go back from it. It wasn't long before I moved from snorting heroin to injecting heroin intravenously. I started hanging out with gang members. I would make nightly drives from NW Indiana to the projects of Chicago, IL just to buy more heroin. I would park my car in a horrible part of town, turn off all the lights, but keep the car running and wait while the person I was with, who went into the projects to buy the drugs, would come back. I was scared. Every single time, I was scared. I kept going anyway.

In time, I got sick and tired of being sick and tired. I would have to take heroin just to feel normal, just to function properly. I wanted to stop; I didn't know how. I asked people how to stop, how horrible the detox was. I was familiar with detoxing off drugs and alcohol, I just knew detoxing off heroin would be intense. I learned it would take three days. Three days and three nights of hot flashes and cold sweats. Vomiting, diarrhea and headaches. It sounded horrible, but I was ready.

I went to my parents' house. I didn't know where else to go. By this time, they were pretty much done with me, but they allowed me in to sleep. The cold sweats started. I couldn't handle it. I called an old AA sponsor and told her what I had done. She asked if I told my parents. I said no. She told me I had to. I said no. She called my parents and told them what I was going through. My mom walked into my room and asked me to roll up my sleeves and show her my arms. I didn't want to. I cried. I told her no. She refused to leave until I showed her. I lifted my shirt sleeves and she saw all my track marks. She shook her head at me, and I saw how disappointed she was in me. She left the room. I had never felt more ashamed in my life.

My ex-AA sponsor left work early, came and got me and took me to the psych ward where they were able to help me detox. They offered me a barbiturate to help me sleep the first night but told me the next two nights I would be cold turkey. This facility did not advocate methadone or any other kind of weening medications.

I remember on the second day the doctor coming in and telling me I was going to be transported to inpatient rehab the next day. I told her I wasn't going. She looked me dead in the eyes and told me then I was going to die. I decided then and there I was going to find a way out of this. I had been walking this road of AA, NA, prescriptions, therapy, inpatient drug and alcohol rehabilitation, outpatient drug and alcohol rehabilitation and doctors for years. It wasn't working for me. I had tried these things wholeheartedly for periods of time at this point, but I still couldn't connect. I was discharged from the facility within the next day or two and I could barely walk. It would take me 30 minutes just to walk up one flight of stairs. I would have to place both of my hands around the tops of one thigh, pull it up, place it on the stair in front of me then switch to the other leg and pull it up and repeat this over and over until I was up the stairs.

I went to AA, AGAIN. I fell off track with alcohol, AGAIN. In September of 2005, I got my third DUI. I totaled my car. I lost my job. I lost the support of good friends and family. I, again, found myself in the psych ward for attempting suicide. My third DUI held a much stiffer penalty. I was looking at becoming a felon, spending a year in jail and losing my driver's license for the rest of my life. My parents, out of the kindness of their hearts, took me into their home one last time. There was one condition - I had to have a job. I had to make the biggest decision of my life. I had to choose to live or I had to choose to die. I chose to live.

Within three blocks of my parents' home was a health food store where I got hired. I was hired and started my first day of work on the same day as my grandmother's funeral. Another family member's funeral I missed because of the poor choices I had made. It was at this health food store that my life began to change for the better. My wish and desire of trying to find the answer to save my life, started to unfold. I learned how important protein was to health and healing. I understood carbs and sugar in new ways. In time, I learned the five things that if all people were aware of, most lifestyle disease could be reversed. I was my own guinea pig for years. I studied the human body non-stop until a very clear picture was downloaded into my brain.

The five things I learned were:

1. To watch sugar and carbs. These types of foods cause the pancreas to produce too much insulin. Too much insulin caused the blood sugar roller coaster. The blood sugar roller coaster caused people to feel tired. When people feel tired, what do they reach for? More sugar and carbs! Alcohol turned into sugar in the body.

2. Candida. Candida is a type of yeast that lived in the human body. When in harmony with the human body, all is well. However, candida is a living organism. What do living organisms need to survive? Food! Candida lives on sugar. When the body has too much sugar in it, then candida is having a field day, bingeing on sugar. When candida binges on sugar it overgrows. What do people do when they are hooked on sugar? They eat more sugar. A vicious cycle unfolds.

3. Inflammation. When candida is overgrown and running rampant, it gets into the blood stream. When in the blood stream, it starts to affect the body at the cellular level-the cells. What do the cells contain? Our DNA. In time, too much sugar, creates too much candida, which turns on each person's inflammation marker's in their cell's DNA. What disease markers are found in each person vary based on their lifestyle, ancestry, ethnicity and a variety of other markers.

4. Digestive Distress. Once inflammation is occurring, it starts to affect the digestive system. Stress can only be handled for so long before one thing starts to affect the next, just like the domino effect. Foods people once love become harder and harder to digest. Add excess stress and worry into the mix and in time, serious gut health issues will occur.

5. Adrenal Fatigue. We arrive here. The human body's stress response. I put adrenal fatigue at the end, but this whole circuit I found was a circle. What comes first? Adrenal fatigue or sugar/carb overload?

Let's take a little look here at human history, how many generations back can you see stress and/or worry affecting your family? Genetics play a huge role health. The amount of stress your mom and dad, your grandparents, your great-grandparents, etc. were under got passed down your genetic coding and can affect your DNA too.

The human body only knows how to keep us alive, that's what the Central Nervous System (CNS) is for, keeping us alive. The CNS is rudimentary. It's about fight or flight, live or die. The body doesn't understand the difference between us being chased by a lion or us being cut off in traffic. To the body, it's the same stress. It loads up a fear signal that gets sent up the spine, to the brain, the brain thinks you are dying, sends a signal back down the spine to the adrenal glands, the adrenal glands emit the hormone cortisol into the body so you don't have a heart attack and that pattern continues over and over and over. Now, take a moment and think about how many times a day you get stressed out. How hard do you believe your CNS is working?

These were the things I did, to calm down my body's stress response:

- ate high vibrational food. Food that made me feel light, fit and energized, instead of food that made me feel weighed down.
- drank adequate amount of water. People should shoot for half their body weight in ounces of water per day.
- got adequate sleep; 7-9 hours is the average amount of time people need to restore their body's energy reserve.
- took deep, cleansing breaths from the belly, not the lungs. These deep breaths told the CNS to calm down, everything is ok, you're safe.

After I learned to heal on the physical level, things went well for a while. In time though, I found myself falling off track for short periods of time and going back to drinking. Occasionally I would add drugs back in as well; I never used heroin again once I detoxed from it and recovered.

Something was missing. I didn't know what for years. Then one day I realized I was missing this whole mental, emotional and spiritual part. The deep cleaning. The root cause of my issues. The things I didn't even know needed cleansing. These included, fear, shame and guilt.

I worked at that health food store for nearly 13 years and only two people knew of my past. I was so ashamed of the person I once was; I kept my secret hidden. I learned that shame hides in secrecy and that's what I truly was, ashamed. I was still stupid, fat and ugly. I was a nobody that no one wanted. I was still broken and lost. Fear was my best friend for years. I was afraid of what others would think of me. I was afraid of breaking free and just being me. I honestly didn't know that was even an option. So, I lived in not good enough for years.

One day, I woke up. Out of the blue. It was very fast, and I honestly had no idea what was happening to me. I went to school to become a health coach and as they were teaching me how to work with clients, a new way of BEING was formed. I started to write again. I couldn't stop. There was so much coming up and out of me and at an exponential speed. I didn't know what was happening. I didn't have anyone to ask. I wrote letters of apology to people. I wrote letters to people around old memories. I wrote and I wrote and I wrote and I wrote because I hadn't allowed myself to write in years.

I knew beyond a shadow of a doubt I was going to be a good health coach because of all my life experience. One day, I did the scariest thing imaginable to me and I told my story three different times to my co-workers at that health food store. The store had three stores at the time and the owner allowed me to share what my new business was going to be about. My health coaching school told me that the most important tool I had was my story. I took that to heart. I was scared, but I told my story. Every single employee walked away differently that day I shared.

I had finally broken free from the prison of my own mind out loud for the first time ever to a crowd of people. Never in a million years would I have thought I would become a public speaker. Ever. In fact, in college I was so terrified of public speaking class. I would go to the bar before my speeches and drink one or two beers to calm myself down. That was hard for an alcoholic like me to do, considering once I took one sip I drank until I passed out.

I took one step in front of the other to build my business. I realized that the re-curing dreams I had since I was seven years old about having hundreds of acres of land where people came to learn about health, a space I called "The Village", a retreat center, was a vision. It took someone a lot smarter than me to point that out. In the same dream I saw myself leading lots of people up a mountain. At that young age I was frightened. I saw it as Revelations, end of times. What I know it as today, is new beginnings.

The very first talk I gave, Discover Total Well Being, brought in about 33 people. I gained two paying clients immediately after that talk, no questions asked. They put down a deposit and scheduled their appointments. I was scared and my voice shook, but I gave that talk. I pushed through and gave more talks.

Now, I get approached to speak and I find places to schedule talks. It's a blessing to be of service to others. I still have fear when giving my talks, but the fear is not as strong as it once was.

I've also become a #1 Amazon Best-Selling Published co-author in the Women In Business division. I am a course creator, a Certified RMT, have clients all over the world, host women's healing retreats, make new friends and alliances, started a second business and help other spiritually gifted entrepreneurs become confident business owner's as well. One day a friend pointed out The Next Impactor competition to me. I thought, why not? My health coaching school told me my most important tool was my story and I believed them. So, I joined the competition and my world expanded and grew even bigger.

I was chosen to be a part of the top 50 impactors with Coach Vicky Omifolaji and nine other women who became soul sisters. Each of their missions touching my heart and allowing me to expand and grow in ways I could have only dreamt of. My life, again, forever changed by this gift.

I'm not quite sure where my path will go next friends, but I've learned to stay in the moment. How I once viewed life as painful and devastating I now see as beautiful and full of many empowering choices.

I desire to share ten more powerful things with you friends. These are the 10 Tips to Your Best Life. These are the Ten things I connect to EVERY DAY to keep me moving forward. In just two years, I've been able to accomplish things that take a lot of people their entire life to create. I share with you because I believe in you. You are the most important person there ever is. Who you are, matters. You are the only you that will ever be born, and I encourage you to be the very best version of you that you can possible be. Everyday: without fail.

I love you. I believe in you. If you are lost, I am a guide the Universe has sent to guide you on your journey.

Ten Tips to Your Best Life

1. Decide

   Be honest with yourself when making decisions.

Do you want this habit changed more than anything or do you just like the idea of it?

2. Become Good Enough

   Perfectionism kills the idea every time.
   Learn to be okay with your "good enough" for the day.

3. Be In The Moment

   Connect to your breath, find the stillness, listen for the answer.

4. Recognize Your Own Energy Reserve

   Are you giving from a tank that is full or a tank that is empty?
   Only give to others what you deem as "extra".

5. Never Give Up

   If it looks like failure is inevitable, find another route.
   Remember to ask for help.

6. Become Grateful

   Gratitude raises your vibrational level and wins EVERY SINGLE TIME!

7. Make Your Habit Change Bigger Than Your Fear

   People talk themselves out of things all the time. Make your new wish for your habit change non-negotiable, then you will totally follow through.

8. When It Seems Like Everything Is Falling Apart On You, Focus On Your Health

You have control over yourself, not life's circumstances. When life happens, (and oh, it will) focus on what you can do to improve your own health.

9. Become Daring

    You cannot have the habit change you are seeking if you continue to play it safe. Be daring! Try something new.

10. Find the Joy!

    If you make your new habit "work" it will not stick.
    Find the joy in what you are doing and watch the magic happen.

Chapter 4

TIAUNA ROSS

Tiauna Ross is a Michigan-based professional, career and empowerment coach. She is also an author, speaker and trainer, who actively works with individuals and groups to improve personal effectiveness through career coaching, mentoring, seminars, training and personal development.

Tiauna has achieved great success in the areas of accounting, technology and project management. She has over 15 years of experience in finance and accounting, project/program management, business and systems analysis, communication and change management. Tiauna is known for her innovative and resourceful approach to managing people, projects and systems and her reputation for helping others achieve career and personal success. She has led many award-winning multi-million-dollar projects throughout her career and has written articles for the PM Times, the BA Times and LinkedIn. She is a co-author of the book "Positioned to Prosper". As a speaker she has delivered keynote addresses for the Michigan Association of CPAs, the Power of We Symposium (Chicago and Atlanta) and has been featured on numerous podcasts and shows, most recently featured on MTV.

Tiauna earned a Master of Science degree in Accountancy and a Bachelor of Business Administration degree, majoring in Accountancy & Personal Financial Planning, both from Western Michigan University. She completed the Stanford Advanced Project Management program in 2013 and is a Stanford Certified Project Manager, a Certified Public Accountant, a Certified Business Analysis Professional, and a Project Management Professional. She is also a Certified Human Behavioral Consultant and a Certified 5D Coach through the Authentic Identity Institute.

Tiauna is a member of the Project Management Institute, the International Institute of Business Analysis and the Michigan Association of CPAs where she is a contributor on the Program Curriculum and

Membership task forces. She is also the Vice Chair of the Management Information and Business Show task force.

Tiauna is the founder of Elevated Execution LLC. She can be contacted at info@tiaunaross.com.

I want to first express gratitude to a power higher than myself for giving us all the power of choice. I am thankful for that power. Being able to choose, is a privilege and what we do with it is completely up to us. In one of the most famous books of all time, the Bible, there is a story about how the first man and the first woman were given a choice and according to this book, they chose wrongly. When I first heard this story as a kid sitting in church, I remember thinking to myself, "Why would God give them a choice, knowing that they would choose to go in the wrong direction?" However, as I grew older and broadened my knowledge, I have come to realise that choice is a gift. In fact, in looking at religious texts from all around the world, I was able to find one thing in common – the power of choice. Because not even a higher power can take away your power of choice. We are all here on this planet, at this time, to choose for ourselves.

It is the power of choice that has brought all of us to this moment in our lives, to become the people we see when we look in the mirror each and every day. This power, whether we use it to build or destroy, to set free or to place in captivity, the power of choice is something that we all use to sculpt our very existence – whether we acknowledge it or not and whether we are aware of it or not.

I didn't always understand this; but what I can say is, acknowledging and using the power of choice has been instrumental in helping me achieve success in my life and also has been crucial in the work I do to help others achieve success in their lives. To date, I have been fortunate enough to travel the world, earn multiple college degrees and multiple certifications. I'm a published author, speaker, and career coach who has managed a number of multi-million-dollar award winning projects and helped countless others achieve their goals. In short, I am a woman who has succeeded against the odds of growing up black in one of the inner cities of America.

I am from a small town in Michigan called Benton Harbor. I am old enough to remember what life was like in a poor black neighborhood in America in the early 1990s, but I was too young at the time to fully understand it. As a child, I witnessed a sharp increase in crime in our neighborhood, which also marked the beginning of the crack epidemic in Black neighborhoods all across the country. In the span of just one year, our neighborhood became a place that no longer held the safety we'd previously known. People were breaking and entering to steal televisions and electronics out of homes, stereos and music equipment out of cars, kid's bikes began disappearing from front yards. Even in a small town like ours, the same gangs that plagued big cities like Los Angeles, had found their way into our city and were fighting a bloody war in the streets, earning our town the heavyweight title of "the murder Capital of America". Gunshots were heard on a regular basis, so much so that people were no longer startled to hear the sound of gunfire. Adults became fearful about kids playing outside too much or too far from home and when one young girl's body was found in a dumpster after a city-wide search, their fears were made evident.

My mother used to be very, very careful, taking extra safety precautions. I thought she had gone too far when she started pulling out all of our kitchen drawers to block the back door at night. I remember being at home late one night, at nine years old, when I heard the sound of glass shattering at our back door and wondered what was going to happen next. I crouched low on the kitchen floor, frozen and gripped with fear, as I watched an arm reach inside the broken back door window to unlock it. Luckily for us, that night my mother had pulled out those drawers behind our back door before going to her third shift job. As the door opened and hit the barrier, my aunt, who'd crawled next to me, yelled out, "I have a gun and I've already called the police. They are on their way right now. Leave now, or I'll have to shoot you." The truth was, the police weren't on their way and we didn't have a gun. It was only me, my little brother and my aunt, a woman who didn't have a violent bone in her body. Even though I was physically shaking, I felt a sense of relief when the arm pulled back through the window and we heard the back-porch screen door close. Eventually, the police did come. If the door had not been blocked by my mother's extra safety measures, I can't begin to wonder what kind of a crime scene they would have shown up to.

Unfortunately, poverty has a way of seeping into areas where you least expect its impact. I still remember the night my mother called me into her room to talk to me. I knew it was serious. I tried to think of what it could be. As I walked up to her room, I tried to replay my day, wondering if I'd done something that would get me into trouble. Unable to think of anything, I entered her room.

"Tiauna, I have to go away for a while." She paused for a long time, trying to think of what to say next. "Do you know what rehab is?"

"Rehab is short for rehabilitation. It's where people go to recover from drugs."

"You're so smart. You have always been so smart." Her eyes filled up with tears. She hugged me and cried. "I am so sorry. I have to do this to become better. I promise you I will get better. I will come back better. It's just for a little while. I love you and I want to do what's right by you and your brother."

As I stood there, the seeds of self-doubt grew inside, and I just nodded. But when she left, and I had to explain to the other neighborhood kids where she'd gone, I felt unsure. It was like the least little bit of confidence I had in myself left me when she did. The same woman who'd tried so hard to make sure I make the right choices was gone; she had fallen into one of the traps in our environment. I wasn't sure whether I would fall too.

All around me, it seemed life was unpredictable. I second guessed myself, my value as an individual, my instincts. Life appeared to be random, problems seemed bigger than life and at times, I seemed small – too small to matter. There were many things in that situation that I did not have control over. For a short period of time, I felt like I didn't have any real choices. But one right choice can lead to so many resolutions.

My mother had her own struggles, but she was adamant about one thing. She would make sure I understood the importance of getting an education and that I had what I needed to pursue it. When I was in elementary school, one of my teachers told her I was very smart and recommended a school for academically gifted and talented children. My mother did everything necessary to get me enrolled. It was good for me to be in a small setting where the teachers could understand each kid's differences and had the ability to adjust the materials. They expected a lot from us and we performed to their expectations. I remember being engaged and challenged in that environment. I really believe attending this school gave me something to focus on, to keep my mind occupied.

I was very independent as a student. The assignments I received from the school awakened a desire to find answers to difficult questions. I spent a lot time looking for answers on my own and reading any and everything I could get my hands on. After a while, my aunt decided it was time to take me to the library to keep me geared towards reading books, and probably to stop me from reading everything else. It was by reading books that I realized there was a whole world out there, bigger than what I could see at that time and I knew in my heart that more was waiting for me.

I started to read the biographies of people like Nelson Mandela, Sojourner Truth, Harriet Tubman, Martin Luther King Jr., Marcus Garvey and Thurgood Marshall. I started to understand what the generations of African Americans before me had gone through and how they continued to believe and tried to make the best choices they could, even with everything around them pressing upon them to give up on themselves and their hopes. They too had people, places and circumstances that tried to steal away their power of choice, even the simple choice to believe in freedom, equality and a better future. I started to understand that I was a continuation of the people who'd survived the Transatlantic Slave Trade, the brutality of slavery, the unfairness of Jim Crow. I thought about my grandmother, who'd left the south with nothing but hope and made a life for herself, even when her own father said she'd never amount to anything. I looked at my own mother, who I watched worked on her hands and knees, remodelling the bathroom of our home after working 12-hour shifts, because she wanted to get us a home in a better neighborhood. She chose to believe she could, and she eventually did. It was there that I discovered the power of choice.

I developed a sense of confidence in knowing that I could decide what I was going to do, what I was going to believe and who I was going to be. But just because you make choices for yourself and believe in yourself doesn't mean that you won't be shaken. Sometimes the choices that we overlook the most are the choices that are impressed upon us. Let me say this in a different way, the choices you are least aware of are the ones that are suggested to you.

One of the first choices I made for myself was that I would become the very first person in my family to graduate from college. I saw this as my ticket to a better life and I was determined to follow this choice through.

When I was in high school, I interned at a large company. I won't name any names but there was a man there, who was an engineer, and he was granted patents, which means his inventions were used in products. I don't even know if the other people in that group of kids even remember this, but one day, he gathered all of us in the conference room and told us the following: "At the high school that you all go to your A's are like C's everywhere else. I studied at Purdue and I struggled for C's there. How do you think you're going to do in college? What do you think is going to happen to you when you go to college?"

I'd already decided that I was going to college and not only that, I was determined to be a top student. I had to work hard in high school for the good grades that I had. I knew my high school wasn't a state-of-the-art facility. I knew we didn't have resources to build fancy computer or science labs; sometimes we didn't even have enough books. His struggle to make it in college had nothing to do with what struggles I would face or whether I was prepared to go through my own journey.

I could have taken that suggestion and said to myself, "if it was hard for him, what makes me think I'm going to succeed in college? I don't know anybody who has become an engineer. It's going to be harder for me because I'm not getting the same opportunities to learn as others are. I might as well give up here." His comments may have shaken me if I hadn't seen what I'd seen, read what I read, been through what I'd already been through. I may have doubted myself. I may have reconsidered my choices. He'd been somewhere I'd never been, but I'd also been somewhere he'd never been. See, when you've seen the low points of life, when you've set your mind on better, and the only thing driving you forward is confidence that you can make things better if you bet on you, there's nothing that can be done to shake you down from who you've fought so hard to become. Maybe you don't have to just believe and choose your way out of the very bottom, but I had to. And if it hasn't happened in your life yet, just keep living, it will.

Somebody else in that room may have chosen differently. Just because someone suggests to you that you can't make it, that no one's ever done what you're trying to do, that people from where you're from don't go certain places, don't do certain things, doesn't mean you don't have a choice. I can suggest anything to you but it's your choice to believe it or not. You can accept it, or you can throw the whole conversation away and say I'm going to be the one to make it.

You have to be aware of the choices you have. Just because something is on the menu, doesn't mean you have to order it. Don't let someone else trick you out of your choice because, like I said in the beginning, not even God does that. The universe, higher power, the creator is not tricking you out of your choice. It's all up to you how you proceed. It's still your choice.

I started ninth grade with about 700 other kids. There were a lot of kids in ninth grade with me because all the kids from the three junior high schools attended the same high school in my hometown. I graduated with 205 seniors from my high school. Now what happened to the other five hundred kids? I don't know for certain. A number of them transferred to other schools in surrounding communities. Some of them moved away. Others completely dropped out altogether. A few of them were incarcerated. Tragically, some of my classmates died before they could make it to graduation. What made me think I was going to be number six out of 205 kids? In the bigger picture, I was really number six out of the 700 who started high school with me. It was simple. I knew I couldn't make it to college without making it through high school.

And since I was going to college, dropping out of high school was never a choice for me. I couldn't focus on who on the left side or the right side, went to another school, moved away, quit, became incarcerated or died. Rest in peace to all the classmates I lost along the way, gone but not forgotten. I chose to keep moving forward against the odds and that is what the power of choice is all about.

When I was in college, three major life events occurred that could have caused me to quit. In April 2004, I got married. In August 2004, I got pregnant. I hadn't completed college yet. Now, for many people that would side-track them because getting married is a major life change. Just think about it, two college students, no, two broke college students, getting married and expecting a baby. That's a significant challenge but those were my choices as well.

The third thing was later that year, Mr. LB Anderson, a great man, my grandmother's husband who was like a grandfather to me, became sick. I'd been away at school, studying and working and getting ready to become a mother. I'd been talking to my grandmother and checking in. Mr. Anderson would always ask me how school was going, and he never wanted to discuss his health. He wanted to check to make sure I was focused on my education. When I'd graduated from high school, he was so proud and I remember he looked me in my eyes and made me promise I was going to go to college, be the best I could be and finish. It was an opportunity that he and my grandmother could only have dreamed of for themselves and I was getting ready to make it a reality.

Whenever I called, he only wanted to hear all about how school was going. He wanted to know how I was doing on my exams. He wanted to know if I was managing okay being a pregnant student. I used to tell him that I wish I could come home more. After a while, I would call, and he would be mostly sleeping so I didn't talk to him as much. I didn't make it home until December that year after final exams.

When I walked into the house, he was lying down on the sofa. He could not sit up. He could not hold his head up. His voice was soft and weak.

He'd lost so much weight. I was stunned. The whole time I was away, at school, studying and working, and preparing for my first child, his health was deteriorating. He was dying from prostate cancer; and all that time, he knew but he never told me. He wanted to make sure I stayed focused. I told him I was sorry for not coming sooner. The last thing he said to me before I left was how proud he was that I was doing what I said I was going to do, and he told me to go as far as I possibly could. I promised him that I would not stop, that I would not let anything stop me. He died before the end of the following semester and before my daughter was born. Pay attention to those around you, who believe in you and support you, because most of us only get one Mr. Anderson in a lifetime.

The following school year, my college professors didn't even know I had a baby. I went to office hours one day, pushing my baby in a stroller and one of my professors said, "you have a baby?!" She couldn't tell because I'd been working harder than anyone else. I was at office hours held by the professors. I stayed after class to ask questions. I was getting A's on my exams. I was volunteering as a tutor and showing up at presentations given by employers. Most students, with or without babies, couldn't do all of that very easily. It was not easy, but I knew what my choices were, and I was not going to give up on my dreams.

Right at the very end, I was tested again. I ran out of money the last semester of my undergraduate program. I had only two classes left. It was going to cost me $1,200 to take these two last summer classes to graduate in the summer that year. My situation was straightforward. I didn't have any money. I could not borrow any more money. My scholarship money was already used up. In this case, I chose to move forward. I enrolled anyway. I thought to myself, either the money is going to show up or they're going to kick me out, but I am not going to stop myself. Something or someone else is going to have to stop me but it would not be me who end it here. So I enrolled, even though I didn't have money and I didn't know how I was going to get it. I chose to move forward because I chose to believe. I went to class every day.

My grades were excellent. I did the work assigned to me. Two days before I ran out of time, the most incredible thing happened. I received a phone call from the chair of the finance department. Since one of my majors was personal financial planning, he called me and said, "I see you've applied for a scholarship for the master's degree program and I sit on the scholarship committee. There's a State Farm scholarship that you received two years ago, and we want to give it to you again. You only need to do one thing. Write a letter explaining how it will change your life." I hung up the phone and sprang into action. It took me five minutes to write that letter. That's how I finished my undergraduate program. I did not have a plan but the fact that I chose to move forward toward the future and take a chance on myself paid off for me.

When I made it to graduation day, some people were genuinely surprised. Another graduate turned to me in the line up to go on stage and said, "Wow, you did it." Yes, I did it against the odds, with all fear aside, because it was all up to me. I chose what I wanted to do, and I wasn't going to give anything up; and neither should you.

In closing, I just want to say. Own your choices, that's your power. It was given to you and me by a power greater than we are. It was given to us so we could create the life that we once could only dream of. Good choices lead to good outcomes and poor choices lead to poor ones. At the end of the day, that's your choice, too. You don't have to do good things with your choice because it's yours to do whatever you want to with it. Whatever you do, be mindful of the power that you have, in the things that you choose to do, think and believe. Because it's the power of choice that will shape the rest of your life. Use it wisely.

Chapter 5

Beth Olson

About Beth

Beth Olson is a financial advisor, owner of BFY Choices, and Founder of The Always Feed Piggy Financial Education and Savings Program for Kids. As a leading expert in the field, Beth has helped hundreds of clients take back control of their financial future. Seen by those she works with as "the safe money first girl," Beth helps protect her clients from the volatility and uncertainty of the markets, so they have the financial peace they deserve. Her interest in educating clients on Uninterrupted Compound Interest growth and Opportunity Cost brings a unique perspective to her financial planning practice. Beth is married to the amazing and handsome Mark Olson. She enjoys dancing, hanging with her family, having tea parties and sleepovers with her grandchildren, going to restaurants and chatting with people from all walks of life. You may catch her at a restaurant near you!

Beth can be reached at BFYChoices@gmail.com

My name is Beth Olson. I was born Beth Hasse. Within these pages I will be sharing about me and how I got to where I am now. I am in the first The Next Impactor competition and I'm on a mission to Impact our world for good!

My best childhood memories are the playtimes with my parents. I am second of four children. My brother Bob is the oldest, me, then sisters Barb, and Bonnie. My parents, Bob and Bert, were incredible parents. Strict, yet extremely loving in so very many ways, playful, and they taught each of us a lot and allowed us to grow in our own ways.

We attended church every week except when we were camping or out of town. My dad was the superintendent of the church school. My mom and dad were both teachers in the Sunday school and my brother, myself and sister also started teaching after we made our confirmations in the eighth grade. When I was younger, I would go around the neighbourhood to teach the other kids whose parents weren't able to take them to church, about Jesus. Since I had access, I would use the extra Sunday school materials that dad didn't use in his class.

We camped nearly every weekend in the summers. We also had huge campouts in our backyard for the neighborhood once a year, and dad would cook for everyone and set up a long table on the driveway for everyone to eat at. Our house was usually the neighborhood playhouse. We played pretty much every kind of outside game you can think of in the yard, and also had a swimming pool, so you know everyone came over for that too! Camping trips were always way too fun! I loved being outdoors all day, fishing, hiking, playing, swimming, walking our dogs. Every weekend camping trip was a magical time for us…mom may not agree, though, since she always did all the packing and cleaning up. Dad always spoiled and loved her immensely which made up for it and gave all of us kids a great impression to desire for our future relationships.

Back at home on weeknights, you'd find the neighborhood playing hide and seek usually. The other parents got used to dad and the older boys hopping fences. The other parents knew it was just all of us having fun and dad was keeping all the kids active while having fun. For the times we couldn't play outside, dad made sure we pretty much had every possible toy. All the other kids called our basement the "Mini Bargain Town", which was a very large toy store at that time; it became Toys 'R Us.

I was also so very fortunate to have my best friend live right next door to me. When I was born, she was six months old and we became besties as young as day one for me. Now just so we're all clear, she is older than me; I tease her every year on her birthday, so you know I'm going to do it here. Helen is my lifelong friend literally. Though she now lives in another state, we remain close due to the magic of social media and the technology we now have in our world. We are to this day in contact nearly every day. Having my best friend living next door to me was awesome. To say my childhood was blessed is an understatement….and I wouldn't trade it for anything.

As my thoughts turn to the topic of the most defining moments in my life, I know that those moments have names…my children…Tony, Daniel, Ricardo, Eric, Crystal and my heavenly daughter who was before all of my born children. I only knew her for 13 short weeks inside of me. I loved her and of course still do, but I never got to see or hold her except within me. It broke my heart as I tried so hard to have my body hold onto her, but just couldn't do anything more but lay in bed hoping and praying for the outcome I wanted for her. It was an incredibly dark and horrible time for me to get through. We don't know why and aren't meant to know in this world the why, but I know she's with me and is waiting for me and I will meet her one day.

You can only imagine how ridiculously elated I was when I got pregnant again seven months later with my first born. I was so careful during the entire pregnancy with everything I ate and did. I was blessed with Tony a beautiful, healthy son born to me. Eighteen months after Tony was born, we were blessed with Daniel. Two years later the blessing of my son Ricardo, and two years after him, the blessing of my son Eric. So, within six years I had four of my children. Four years after Eric, I was blessed with a daughter. She was meant to be named Christina because she was due around Christmas. But when she was born and Tony saw her, he asked if we could name her Crystal because she was so precious and beautiful. By the age of 28 I had all of my children. I have a total of five children born, each of them with their own personalities and gifts. I cherish each one of them as the gifts they are and I am so happy God gave them each to me. It's amazing how very different they are even though they were raised the same way. God has special plans for each of them, though, so they have to be different. As I raised them, and continue to even as they are adults, there are two poems I always keep in mind and keep posted in my home. The titles of those two poems are: Children Learn What They Live by Dorothy Law Nolte, Ph.D. and If I Had My Child to Raise Over by Diane Loomans.

Children are given to us on loan to do the best we can for them. We can only do the best we can with the tools we have. We get these kind of life tools from our own upbringing, other areas of our life such as friends and family, experiences we have been exposed to and education. So the best thing we can do is equip ourselves with as many positive tools as we possibly can while raising our children...the future of our world.

It's important that we know we have the power to make the right choices, especially when it comes to raising our children. Children truly are gifts from God. We all are gifts to this world. Unwrap the gift you are and give yourself to the world as God intended.

A few of the things I have learned along the way that I really want to share with the younger generation is to Love, live, be happy, share, make memories, be thankful, Love, and about uninterrupted compound interest. Yes, I wrote Love twice...and on purpose. I have learned throughout my life, that All of Life truly is Love. If we can know this and look at every part of life from the glasses of love, life will not only be much easier for us, but it'll also make for a better world. Obviously, and sadly, everyone else won't be looking through those glasses, but it will make our lives easier if we can remember to do this. Again, All of Life is Love.

Another is to live. Get out into our fantastic world. There are so many experiences and adventures waiting for you. Don't get bogged down with living someone else's life that is on the tv, on a DVD, or on the news. This is your life. We all are here in this time and get this time... and we don't know how long that time is. Get out there and meet others, help others, make friends, get involved, share your knowledge, pet, play and take care of pets. In other words, stop and smell the roses…and grow some while you're outside.

Be happy. Always look on the positive side of things. Looking to the negative puts you in a funk that's often times difficult to get out of. Life is too short to not be happy. When you get to your end, you will not be thinking of the unhappy moments, you will be thinking of the happy ones and wishing you had more time to have and make more happy moments. So, stay happy as often as possible.

Share yourself with others. You will learn so much throughout your life. You already, at any given moment, are who you are meant to be and are equipped at that moment with what you are meant to know. Go out into the world and share yourself. It could be in knowledge, it could be your time spent with someone, it could be time spent with animals to help them, it could be to plant something to enrich our world. Whatever the time is, get out there and share yourself. It will come back to you ten-fold however you choose to share. Just share you. We are put together in this time to help each other.

Make memories every day. Start each year with a fresh new journal. Be sure it has at least 365 blank pages. Every single day at the end of the night, write down a special memory you made that day.

Also write down what your goal for the next day is. By making a special memory every day and writing it down, you will have a lifetime of awesome memories to look back at to brighten your day. Remember, memories don't have to be extravagant, just something or things you do each day to make your day special. Each day is a special gift and is worthy of special moments that should be recorded. Your future family will cherish them, and hopefully you will instil this practice into all members of your family too!

Be Thankful always for everything. Even when you think there is no reason to be thankful, there is. Even when it's been a bad day, there is always something within that day to be thankful for. It could be the lesson learned that day to be thankful for. And when you recognize that, often times, you won't need to go through learning that lesson again. If it does happen again, be thankful for the reminder.

Uninterrupted Compound Growth. That's a mouthful. But having it work on your side can and will make a significant difference for your financial future. However, if it's working against you… it's really not good. So, know this. As you take on your financial world, be sure you are always having your money work in the realm of Uninterrupted Compound Growth. Most financial vehicles put you in the realm of what they call Compound Growth. It sounds wonderful. Einstein talked about it after all. The piece that is left out when he is quoted, however, is the Uninterrupted part. Once the chain of Compound Growth is broken, you start over. To make Compound Growth work in the most advantageous way for you, it must be Uninterrupted. Loans and credit cards are examples of Compounding working against you. Be very careful with these as you take on your financial world.

If I could have done one thing differently in my life, I would say it would have to be that of learning about Uninterrupted Compound Growth early on in my life instead of in my later years. Unfortunately, no one in "my world" knew about it to teach it to me. No one knew about this or the vehicles that can be used to get the most bang for your buck with it either. We don't know what we don't know and then we can't teach it either. This is why I have made it my life's work now to share information about this to everyone who is willing to listen and learn.

Had I had this knowledge years ago, let alone when I was very young, I could have taught it to my own children early on too. It would have made an immense different in our financial lives. Compounding works best with time on your side. But as I tell everyone, today is your youngest day and possibly your healthiest day also. So, don't waste today.

Learn about Uninterrupted Compound Growth and learn about the best vehicles to grow it in for you at the age you are. It'll make a significant difference for your future. Don't wait. Learn about it as soon as you can and teach it to others. The more we can share these important matters, the better it is for everyone!

I'd love to share with you something that helps me get through each day. Learn to have the Attitude of Gratitude. I start my day and end my day with what I'm grateful for. That gratefulness starts with thanking my God for the day and the gift of life and the possibility to do something good every day for someone. He gives us the power of choice each day, to do what we want with our time. It's up to each of us to choose what we'd like to do, but he gives us nudges for what he wants us to do if we listen.

We all have a purpose for being here. I choose to try to fulfil God's wants for my life since he knows what my purpose is. It's not always easy to listen with all of the 'noise' that is constant in the day, but I try. I am so grateful for his presence, patience and guidance. I am also so grateful for my husband, Mark. He is my rock, love, best friend, and partner. To have someone to hang out with in all ways, even when we are bored, makes life so much sweeter. Mark has brought much joy to my whole family and has really shown myself, kids and mom a whole new world. He loves making sure whomever we are with is having a good time. He's a very giving man and has many stories and jokes to share and enjoys seeing how people react to his jokes. It makes me laugh every time I hear him start one of his jokes because I know his body language when he's getting ready to start one. He loves to make people laugh. Mark is also an incredibly hard, strong worker who takes much pride in his work and he's very good at what he does. He has taken on the role of friend to all of my adult children and grandfather to our grandchildren. Watching him over the years grow into his role of grandfather has been heart-warming to all of us. He never had children of his own. So babies, diapers, tons of toys, crying, and all of the joy of little ones has been amazing to watch him adjust to. We all have so much love and admiration for him. We are so blessed to have found each other!

My children, Tony, Crystal, Daniel, Ricardo, Eric, and daughter-in-love Sarah, along with my grandchildren, Sebastian and Harrison are truly my heart and I am so incredibly grateful for having each of them in my life. Our home is always most joyous when one, some or all of them are visiting. We enjoy having dinners, movie nights, playing, dancing, and campfires together. There are so many laughs when we are together. We go to many places together including family vacations. I am always so grateful for those times to create memories together that do last a lifetime. No time to rest, gotta fest. And it's always so much more fun with each other.

Our family really enjoys going to the Renaissance Faire at least one time per season. We look so forward to that day. We plan the date when everyone can make it due to work schedules. We go on that date whether it is a day of rain, shine, cold, hot, ridiculous humidity, we just go. We've been through every type of Midwest weather while there except snow…only because it is a summer only event. And, of course, the costumes. We plan those well in advance and are always on the lookout for new pieces to add to our Ren Faire attire all year. It's just a fun day when we can just go and enjoy being together with no agenda but always with lots of laughs. A lot of our friends meet up on the same day also, so we are always bumping into familiar faces too. It's just a ton of fun and we all look so forward to it. Even the grandkids are crazy about it. They start practicing their "old English" accents days prior. Though it's not terribly hard for them since they were both born in England and they have natural English accents.

Another significant thing we do together is Family pizza and movie night, every Friday night. Everyone enjoys the special time together at the end of the week. It's a great time for all of us to wind down from the week. We share what has happened throughout the week, eat pizza and try to watch a movie. Having four dogs running around and playing and everyone chatting, sometimes hinders watching of the movie. No matter though, it's just being together that we all really enjoy. Sometimes pizza night is at our house, sometimes it is at my son Eric's house. It's quite the treat at Eric's house though. He has a huge outdoor pizza oven and is always trying new dough recipes out on us. It's a very active hour or so as pizza dough is being hand tossed and we each top a pizza in our own special ways. Friday pizza night has been part of our lives since my kids were little. I'm happy it is still a tradition that we all enjoy together. Pizza and family just go together!!

Life is short. You've heard that saying. That's why time with the family is so very important to me. We each have today and really don't know if our day will end being with the one's we love another day. So we have to not waste time. Life is a race against time and time is our most valuable currency. Many believe it is money, but surely it is time. Please don't waste it.

One day, I woke up to learn my oldest son Tony left here to go be with God. To say it was the worst, most horrible day of my life is an understatement. In my mind, it isn't considered a day…it is now my life and my whole family's life. There are no words. Parents should never have to have a child leave before they do. But we can't know why and aren't meant to know the answer as to why in this world.

I knew Tony would leave early…there were messages given to me throughout his short years here, but once he turned 21, I figured it was just me being overly protective. Two weeks later… Another incredibly very dark and horrible time came into my life. I always thought having gone through my miscarriage that I wouldn't have to go through something so horrible again. I have been close to our God since I was a little girl, sharing his teachings, praying for my family and future children and grandchildren and yet this all has happened. I can't understand the why at all, we aren't meant to. I suppose most would have left our God, but he is our God and I know he is always with me and for me. Again, I repeat, I can't understand the why at all, and we aren't meant to.

I miss my son Tony Tremendously…beyond words. To hug him and stroke his hair, hearing his voice and feeling his huge Bear hugs. You know tears are in my eyes as I write this. But I have to share that I do know he's ok. He lets me, my mom and two girlfriends know in his own special ways. Yes, I'd rather have him with me in the way we all know our loved ones to be with us, but he is with us, just in a different way now. He is watching over each of us. He is in God's army. (He let me know this about six months after leaving here.) Tony was undeniably a believer of God.

He taught many through his love the ways and teachings of our God. He was on loan to me from his true father and is now with him fighting for and protecting us. I am so proud and honored to have him as my son. I am so proud of and honoured to have all of my children every day!

There's a special picture I always had in my house. You may know it. It's an Angel watching over two children crossing a bridge. The oldest is the little girl helping the younger brother to cross safely. My Tony and son Danny, when they were little, would tell all of their friends that the angel in the picture was me, their mom.

At Tony's funeral, a friend from across the country had sent a statue of that very picture to the wake. That friend had never been to the house at all and had no way of knowing the significance of it to our family. I was overwhelmed when I saw it. Divine guidance brought that particular statue to me. My little girl who never made it into our world was now crossing her younger brother over the bridge safely.

One day I know I will be with both of them again, along with my dad and all of my cherished family members who have gone before me. I know, even though it's very difficult at times, I need to go on for my family and not waste time. I cherish the time I do have with my children and grandchildren and family and know that God is with me and for me always. I do what I can for him as he whispers to me what he wants.

My philosophy for life is to Love and be love. Do everything you can with the "hat" of love on and in your heart. All of life truly is love. Have love in your heart in every step of your life. Not just with your loved ones, but in every step. With co-workers, people that come into your life even if only for a few moments, animals, plants and the environment, your everyday work, every step wherever those steps take you. When you live with love in your heart, it will affect everyone around you for better and will trickle to others you may never meet. Like the old song says, "What the World needs now, is Love sweet Love". It is still one of my favorite songs because of the intelligent message of those nine words.

Also, treat time as the most important currency you have, because it is. Please do not waste it. Do all you can for good with the time you do have.

A good life to me means having love and being surrounded by family, friends and pets to care for and share life with and having God in the center of all we do. Spending quality time together without distractions hindering our relationships. Being and staying healthy and active, having nutritious foods and sharing in healthy activities that benefit everyone. Having great conversation together with lots of laughs and many hugs. Enjoying meals and conversation together whether at home or a restaurant. Cooking meals together while having great conversation. Doing work that is helpful to and for others that also benefits my family. Having a home for family and friends to come to and feel welcome and comfortable in and to have great conversations, spend time with, and share meals with. Having mine and my family's financial life in order and growing money safely for now and for our futures. Having cars that work well and get us from point A to point B while keeping us safe. Taking vacations together and being able to enjoy the blessings of our world and all that this life has to offer.

Kind of like a dance, I believe life is a series of joyful moments, learning, fun, challenges and setbacks. Two steps forward, one step back, step to the side, slide to the other side, raise your arms in joy, raise your arms in frustration, roll on the floor from despair, jump back up, two steps forward, etc. Many, many steps and experiences. We all have them. These are all the lessons of life that make up our lives. Some of us have what may seem to be more serious challenges than those of others, but we all have our share of them and deal with them differently.

The earlier a person learns the different tools needed to be used for different situations, the quicker a person can get through the challenges and move on. The earlier a person learns to set goals and strategize their life, the easier it is to face the challenges of life and continue through to the goals they desire.

When you connect with your own thoughts and feelings you can perform the actions necessary to get to the results you want. To grow, you need to get out of your comfort zone. You'll reset your personal thermostat each time you get out of your comfort zone. When your choice is to not get out of your comfort zone and stay at the same 'temperature', you stop the potential for growth for yourself and being able to help others. This is fine for some people and some choose to live most of their life living in that comfort zone. That is their choice. We all have the power of choice.

As for me, I go to 'war' with myself. I work against reality of my comfort zone so I can continue to grow so I can serve others. I feel we are all here at this specific time in space to help each other in some way. If I stay in my comfort zone, I won't ever know what else or who else I can help. So what I do is I think about the song "War". I change the words to fit my needs. War, what is it good for, Definitely Something; when I'm working to get out of my comfort zone! Perhaps I'm meant to write songs!

Needing to overcome these challenges and setbacks in order to be truly successful is not something I believe. I believe challenges and setbacks need to be worked through, but they shouldn't stop us from progressing. Perhaps temporarily while fighting through something that you have never dealt with. But not to stop progression until the challenge is overcome. I believe you should continue fighting, even while going through a challenge. We do learn different ways and gain tools throughout life to overcome obstacles. Sometimes we do have the tools to face the challenge head on. That is not necessarily true in every case though. By connecting with others, however, we may learn of someone who can help us get through these challenges. It may be a doctor, dentist, insurance producer, lawyer, teacher, therapist, or coach. A mom, dad, sibling, child, cousin, distant family member, or close family member. Perhaps it's a movie, a song, a piece of art, a sport, or event. By staying connected and not going into a dark hole of a despair, we become aware of others who can help us. Sometimes, helping us is exactly what the other person or object is meant to do. Let others help you when necessary.

Also help others when you can. We are all here at this very specific time in space to help each other.

If I had the power to solve one problem in the world, I would have to say it would be the problem of people not living the life of love toward each other, animals, and our world. If everyone in this world did live the life of love toward every person, we would each stay quiet enough and long enough to hear the other with their thoughts and then problems and differences could be solved easier.

When everyone lives the life of love there won't be any world hunger because everyone would help each other to have food instead of throwing it away and wasting it. We have so many rich resources in our world that go to waste. Much of the reason is due to greed. We have more than enough in our world as far as food and ways to grow it for everyone, and yet we have people going hungry. If everyone lived the life of love that would not happen.

When everyone lives the life of love, there won't be exploitation of each other. When there is love, exploitation in all of its ugly forms will not happen. Living love toward everyone and everything would not allow exploitation.

When everyone lives the life of love, everyone shares instead of hoard. So much more can get done when love is in the equation. The desire to share is strong when there is love.

When everyone lives the life of love, animals are treated fairly and not abused or killed for financial gain. We may be the superior species, but with that power comes very much responsibility toward the animals of our world.

When everyone lives with love toward our world, we respect it and the environment and do the best with the knowledge we have to preserve it for future generations. Whether that be for land, sea or space. Living with love will produce the right decisions for the environment for now and for the future and not for financial gain only.

All of Life is Love. Teach the future generations to live the life of love. By doing so, we could, together, produce World Peace. Live the life of Love in all of your steps in life.

What I see as my purpose in life is that of teaching children. I have been teaching children for most of my life in one capacity or another. It started when I was young and a child myself when I used to teach neighborhood kids about Jesus. Then as I went on to have my own children, I began teaching them not only as a parent would but also the additional teaching that helped them to understand things before, they would enter formal school. Then I went on to run a small childcare. Instead of just babysitting, I taught the children in my care. I knew kids were like sponges so why waste that precious time. Those were some of the happiest years of my life. We did so much together and had so much fun. Watching the children, including my own children, and their eyes light up while growing and learning are times, I will always hold precious in my heart. During those years, I also coached and ran the town cheerleading program in the evenings. After my children were grown, I moved. It was hard going to a new location where I didn't know anyone. Back in my hometown, myself and my kids were very well known because we were involved in so many things. In my new area, I found a church and started volunteering in the nursery. Now I have Grandchildren. I take every opportunity available to teach them life lessons, but especially about saving and managing money. Had I known back in my earlier years the tremendous value of uninterrupted compounding growth; our family path would be very different. It's such a shame that this kind of information isn't taught in schools.

My purpose is to teach this to as many people as possible starting with children so that they can go on to do better things with the money that comes through their hands throughout their lives. We have a terrible crisis right now. Did you know that 100 million adults can't afford a $400 Emergency today? My mission is to eliminate this problem by teaching every child and family to have a full piggy bank in their possession for emergencies. From there on, to teach about money management.

The average person will have over one million dollars that will come in and out of their lives. We want to help them all keep more of that money by learning better ways of managing it and utilizing the magic of uninterrupted compounding. This mission is why I am in The Next

Impactor competition. This mission was whispered to me. I know it was God who whispered it. It is so important to me to get this message and the concepts out to people that it has become my mission and drive every day.

I had just discovered my mission just as The Next Impactor competition began. I almost didn't enter because it was so new. But I decided to go for it because this message and mission are so important to the wellbeing of so many people. No time to waste. Opportunity showed itself and it was time to "just do it". I was chosen to be one of the top 50 of The Next Impactor competition. I was very excited when I heard the news that I was chosen, and it really helped validate the fact that this was a mission and message that needs to get out to the masses and to make an Impact on our world.

The weeks that followed have been amazing. Everything happens for a reason. The team I was chosen to be on in a blind drawing was Team Vicky. Vicky was definitely one of my top choices for my Coach. I was ecstatic when I learned it was her and texted her very quickly with my excitement even while other names were still being drawn for their coaches. Everything happens for a reason. As the drawing went on until the final name was drawn, we discovered everyone on Team Vicky was female! The only team in the competition that worked out this way. Wow! Everything happens for a reason. At our first meeting on the computer with our new team, the notion was given to us by Loren, Co-Founder of The Next Impactor, that these women that were on this team together, who are at the time strangers, will become like sisters and bond together for life. That was no joke! We have all become so close. We span the world in six different time zones and are four generations of women. Amazingly, we have this incredibly strong bond as if we've known each other for years.

I have learned so much through this competition. I am so happy for the impact it has had on my mission in my heart. I have learned confidence, persistence, and the willingness to get out of my comfort zone for a message that is so much bigger than me and serves the greater good. But I have also learned through our incredible Team Vicky, self-awareness, transformation, unification but mostly Love.

Team Vicky truly is Love and We are the Change.

Chapter 6

Antonietta Morrone Birdsell

Biography

Antonietta Morrone-Birdsell was born in the south side of Chicago, Illinois.

At seven years old, she and her family moved to a suburb in Detroit, Michigan called Birmingham. She moved back to the Chicagoland area in 2000 and presently lives in Carol Stream, Illinois, a western suburb of Chicago.

She is a dyslexia advocate and teacher who unlocks children's hidden gifts and potential, being the voice of hope and shining the light on all children by unlocking their GIFT OF DYSLEXIA.

Antonietta has been an elementary teacher for over 25 years in Glen Ellyn, IL and Hazel Park, MI. She has a Bachelor's of Science degree in Elementary Education and a Master's of Science degree in Early Childhood Education. She is presently is in graduate school for her teaching endorsement in Leadership.

Antonietta has been married to her husband, Bruce, the love of her life, for 14 years and has a son, Michael Paul who is 13 years old and a daughter Eliana Pina who is 12 years old. They also have a chihuahua named Lulu and two spotted geckos named Princess and Precious.

Her mission is to be an advocate for the Gift of Dyslexia by being the voice of hope and shining the light on all of the children who share the gift.

My Best Childhood Memory

My name is Antonietta Morrone-Birdsell. I have so many great childhood memories, but my best is one that spans from age 7-18. I was born on the southside of Chicago 52 years ago in 1967. I was the first generation to be born in the United States. My parents and their family came to the United States in the early 1960s. My father, Salvatore Morrone, was born in Motta, Cosenza, Italy and my mother, Pina Tulipano-Morrone was born in Petralia, Sottana, Sicily. They met in Chicago in a school that teaches students to speak English. They were married in 1966, and soon after they got married, they agreed to share a home with my mother's parents, Michael and Angelina Tulipano, since the house had two homes in one, one in the front and one in the back. We lived in the back home and my grandparents and their two children, Lilllian, aged 15 and, Vera, age 19 lived in the front part of the home, for the first six years of my life. My Great Aunt Peppina, my grandmother Angelina's sister and Great Uncle Joe lived next door. My other Great Aunt Maria and Great Uncle Murphy along with their daughter, Antoniette lived a few neighborhoods away as well. We lived an extended family life and it was blissful.

When I turned seven, my father got a job as a lubricating oil chemist in Michigan. The summer of 1974 was when my whole life changed. I went from an extended family setup to a single-family home which included me and my parents, in an apartment located in a Detroit suburb called Birmingham. It was quite a change going from city life into a suburban neighborhood. Though, the town we did move to was very quaint. I adjusted as well as could be but longed for my life as it was. So, in the summer of 1975 after second grade was completed, my mother asked me if I wanted to stay at grandma and grandpa Tulipano's house for the summer, I was so very excited. I missed my extended family that I had left so much and now I had a little cousin Michael who was two years old to play with too. I was so excited to go back. In the neighborhood, I also had made some great friends who I am still in contact with to this day. Looking back, I cannot be sure, but I believe I went back to visit my grandma and grandpa in the summer because my mother worked full time and my parents never believed in strangers babysitting me. Regardless, it all worked out!

So, since my summer of second grade in 1975 through the summer of my junior year in high school in 1984, I shared my summers with my grandparents and aunts. I still have such fond memories of those carefree summer days at my grandma and grandpa's house. As time passed, my aunts did marry and have more children of their own. I often spent a week or two at their houses too, playing with all of my cousins and loving the life of summer!! I loved and missed Chicago so much that in 2000, I moved back; and for the last 19 years I have lived a mile from my Aunt Vera because I wanted to be close to her as I was so many years ago.

My most defining moments in my life:

I have had many defining moments in my life, but the most defining moment that changed me forever was the day my mother died. It happened on May 3rd, 1991 a month to the day after my 22nd birthday. She was 51 years old.

My mother had been very ill, though she had been very strong and stoic about her illness. She had cancer. Her illness began in 1987. This was the year that I went away to college to become a teacher. It was a very bitter-sweet time for me and my father. I was so excited to start my college career to fulfil my mission that had started in first grade, and yet so sad to realize that my foundation was crumbling with my mother being so weak and unable to take care of herself and others like she always had.

She suffered a great deal. I have never been around anyone since then who endured such great pain and anguish. Since the college I attended was only 45 minutes away from home, I would come home every weekend to help my father support my mother, since he needed a lot of help. So, during the week I would act like a normal college kid and by the weekend, I was taking on the role of "mother" to my own mother at age 19. This experience had me grow up really fast, be responsible beyond belief and really appreciate what a caregiver goes through to make sure one's loved one is taken care of to the best of one's ability.

I had very little support in helping my mother. My father was very weak emotionally and the nurses and doctors would always communicate with me. My aunts, my mother's sisters were busy with their families and didn't have much extra time for her and my grandmother was being protected and not told much because she was ill of health. So, this experience really helped me define what it meant to be someone's sole unconditional support. This was the beginning of my journey into caretaking. I seem to be made to care-take. That is what I did best, or so I thought.

Caretaking continued throughout my life. After my mother passed, I took care of my father until he passed two years after my mother. He also had cancer, though unexpectedly died in a car accident one snowy January evening. I tried to be there as much as I could for my grandmother who raised me until her death two years after my mother's, but I was living in Michigan and she still lived in Chicago. Then in 2000, my mother's youngest sister, my Aunt Lilly passed away too young at age 47. I took some time off work to share two weeks with her before she passed and have cherished the time we did spend together. Such tragedy in such a short time really changes a person.

Some might read this and think, wow, how horrific, and yes, I would agree; but through tragedy comes great strength that one never believed one had. It made me very brave. These defining moments in my late teens and early twenties have made me be the calm, cool and collected one in a crisis, the one who often knows what to say to someone who has lost a loved one. I get it. I can sympathize, because I only know too well what it means to go through the unthinkable, unimaginable, horror of losing a loved one before their time to a disease which you have no control over. It makes you hold on tight to those you love and cherish the time you have with them, putting all differences aside. It puts everything into perspective.

Because of my caregiving in my younger years, I now am a hospice volunteer. It gives me great peace to know that I can be that person that I longed to have near me when there was no one to share my pain with. It gives me great peace to know that I can be that "soft place to fall" when one has nothing left to give. I get it, it sucks, and there is nothing you can say to change anything. Sometimes someone needs just a safe place to lay their head and just feel the love of God through someone else's compassionate acts of kindness. It is very cathartic for me. It is so healing to me to know that I have made someone else's day just a little lighter because I was in it.

Strength comes in many forms. Emotional strength is by far a muscle that needs to be strengthened through life experiences. Having a good head on your shoulders also helps because the opposite of strength is weakness. My father and some family members were too afraid to build their emotional muscles. I could have crumbled, but I knew I needed to be there, be the support, the caretaker even at a young age. I guess I was born that way!

What I have learned in my life that I want to share with the younger generation:

I have a frame hanging on the wall in my husband's and my bedroom. I read it every time I walk into our room, I read it when I need strength and I read it to remind me to keep this thought fresh in my mind, I read it because this is the way I believe is the right way to live.

The frame reads as follows: "Accept what is, let go of what was and have faith in what will be."

Easy to read, hard to follow, at times, especially when you have a caring spirit and want to help, fix everyone's problems and make it all better for everyone. This is why I have this frame. To be less of a rescuer and more of an observer and helper ONLY when asked. Over the years of working too hard to please, fix and control the uncontrollable, my pearls of wisdom include this: You can't please enough, fix enough and you certainly can't control anything, or anyone for any extended period of time. It is futile, it is not my job, and it is so much work. It is all based on fear of the unknown, of "making" something happen instead of "letting" it happen. This has been one of my greatest life lessons as of yet.

"Accept what is" to me means let go of your agenda, it is what it is. Whether you agree with what is happening or not, unless you have control to change it, or the circumstance, let it go!

"Let go of what was", this reminds me of those people who hold grudges and bring up the past as a weapon. Again, it goes back to worrying only about yourself, controlling the only thing/one you can control, which is yourself. Be free of the past and put it to rest.

"Have faith in what will be" is a big one, for without faith what do you have; worry, fear, anguish. Believe in the power of intention. Believe in the goodness in life, in people and watch what you can manifest into greatness. You will amaze yourself.

Another lesson that I have learned the hard way is: "Love yourself, think you are worthy, then and only then will others do the same." You are worthy and loved beyond measure. You glow from the inside out. Don't ever let anyone dull your sparkle or dim that light. Joy is the key and love is the fuel.

Finally, my last pearl of wisdom is about the gift of failure. Authors write whole books on failure, everyone, no matter how successful, has failed. As a matter of fact, I believe that the more one fails, the more one is successful. It is not really a question of if one is going to fail, but rather how will one react to failure. Don't give up, its more about finishing the race than giving up in the middle. Failure is not permanent. Rise above it, choose a better path. You got this!

The breakthroughs in my life:

The biggest breakthrough in my life was leaving my full-time teaching position as an elementary school teacher of 25+ years in 2016 to pursue my greatest mission on this Earth, to be a full-time mother to our two children Michael and Eliana. The desire to leave my teaching position of so many years had been percolating since the birth of my second child Eliana in 2007. She was diagnosed with dyslexia in Kindergarten and I have been her advocate and teacher from the beginning. She continues to be my success story and has been my inspiration to join The Next Impactor Season 1. I am sure I am not the only mother who gives to her children more than she has to give at times and my hope is to change the school systems so that each child will receive the proper early interventions and will be taught in a systematic, multisensory, sequential way that is researched based and tried and true to foster success in ALL children.

In being a teacher, I devoted so much time to my students in the classroom that by the time I got home at the end of the day, I was an empty vessel who still needed to give despite having nothing left to share. I still needed to cook, help with homework, focus on Eliana's interventions, while still emotionally supporting our son Michael. My husband, Bruce, often worked nights and weekends, so a lot of responsibility was put on my shoulders. At times, I gave all my best to my students and my own children got the leftovers. This was not right. Deep in my heart I knew this was wrong, but I did not know what to do. I knew something needed to change. The guilt of a working mother and the longing of staying home and nurturing and guiding my children caused me great emotional and physical pain.

The continued giving without refilling led me to a steady decline mentally, emotionally, spiritually and physically. Using the skills I had learned as a young adult, I just plowed through, forged ahead and kept going ignoring all signs of ill health. Again, everything seemed like they were on my shoulders to solve and I believed that I had no help in sight due to my husband's schedule and lack of family support, so I kept plowing through life just existing not thriving.

I had a difficult pregnancy with my son Michael in 2005. There were some uncertain moments, but by the grace of God we did just fine. This was the first time I faced my own uncertain health. It brought up some buried thoughts that resurfaced having to do with my own mother's health struggles. Then ten months later, just like that, I became pregnant again with my daughter, which was planned. I am a teacher and most teachers want to have their babies in the spring so that they can have the summers off. Being the planner that I was and with God's help, this was exactly what happened. She was born in April of 2007. Got to love divine interventions!! During the second pregnancy, I was a little kinder to myself and took better care of us and had a great second run. Actually, I took a two-year maternity leave from teaching and enjoyed spending every minute with my family just being a mom, the best job ever, in my opinion. In 2009, I returned to work, and at this time I began to start to transfer my priorities from my students' success to my own children's well-being. I so loved to do both, but I was not 20 anymore and my body was giving out. This was the first time in my life, at age 42, that I felt limited in my physical abilities. Though I looked fine on the outside, I was falling apart on the inside and was in total denial.

This went on for the next nine years until in 2016, I could no longer function and I had to make a life changing decision to continue working and risk my health, or end my career early and have a drastic life style change. In making this decision to leave, I had to love myself more and prove to myself that I am worthy of such support that I have never allowed myself to have had in the past. This is what I call a breakthrough that was forced down my throat. I went kicking and screaming per se. I was the caretaker, the fixer, the strong one, and now I was not. Talk about surrendering, letting go and letting God. I had a "come to Jesus moment" where I decided to live, to thrive and to break the vicious family cycle of disease. It took two years of healing, and I am so proud to say that I am healthier than ever before. We now have two thriving children, a strong marriage that has weathered a storm and is renewed again. I am a new woman who is ready to make an impact on this world with her second lease on life. Hear me roar!!!

If I could do one thing differently in my life, what would it be.

If I could do one thing differently in my life, I would have worried less and have had more faith. Good thing my life is not over!!! What being forced to surrender to a higher power has taught me is the universe has my back, has your back, has everyone's back. One just has to get out of one's own way. Let go of control, the what ifs, should haves, and could haves and just live a joyful, faith-filled life full of unconditional love expecting greatness. It's that simple!

Easy to say now that I have lived through a lot of mountains and valleys so far in my short, little life. Is this why they say the elderly are so wise? They get it, they have been through the ups and downs. A lot of times, those downs are tough, we feel we have been forsaken, forgotten, punished when it really was just a chapter in the book of life. Turn the page and make chapter two better than chapter one. It is all up to you as to how to live your life. You have free will, choice. Your life is divinely orchestrated. Enjoy your story as it unfolds. Stop trying to make things happen, go with the flow and let it happen.

What am I most grateful for in my life?

What I am most grateful for in my life is my husband, Bruce and my two children Michael and Eliana. They are my greatest blessings; such amazing teachers and I love them unconditionally.

I finally settled on my prince charming late in life. I had many of frogs and finally found my prince when I was 34 years old. We have been married for 14 years and have created many memories. Some memories to be cherished and some to be forgotten, but they were all necessary to add to the creation of our "book of life". Each page of "the book" has so many life lessons, trials, tribulations, joys, blessings and everything in between.

When I met my husband, I knew the second that I met him that we were going to be married. I felt like I had known him all of my life and he has said to me the same thing about our first connection. It was an instant attraction. From the beginning of our relationship we were inseparable.

Within the first year of our marriage, we had our first child Michael. Michael has been such a blessing in our lives. He has brought such joy and promise into our lives since the day he was born. Today, he is a very kind, gentle soul like his father. He is always there willing to help, especially with any tech related issue. This is his strength and love. He is always thirsty for knowledge and an avid reader and podcast listener. He loves to play video games and has a talent of editing videos for himself and his friends. He is a good friend to others and a leader in his group. He likes to take care of other people and help them out when they need him. He is very tall and is an avid cross-country runner and biker. He plays golf and plays basketball with his friends. He is a sweet kid and I don't know what to do without him.

Eighteen months later after the birth of Michael, our daughter Eliana was born. She was our little package of joy. Now our family was complete. God graced us with a boy and now a girl. From the very beginning, Eliana was an easy-going baby and was the apple of our eyes. Today she is 12 years old. She loves to do anything creative whether it be making a stop-motion video on her phone to painting and creating art and dressing up as her favorite characters with her friends from a movie or book she calls anime, to name a few of her passions. She has always loved to dance, and hula-hoop. She runs cross country races, does gymnastics and enjoys biking, like her brother.

They are always thinking of each other and often having each other's back. We have a five-year-old chihuahua, named Lulu and within the year adopted two leopard geckos from our neighbor named Princess and Precious. They are also five years old. Together, Michael and Eliana take care of the feeding and walking of our pets. We love them very much. Having pets has brought much joy and has taught them responsibility. These life lessons of being present for another living being has been very valuable life lessons. They have translated into their own lives, evident in how they tackle their own responsibilities that they have to accomplish. They make us very proud.

When I think of our family as a unit, we have really grown as a united group as time heals old wounds and becomes our greatest teacher. Sometimes the best lessons are the ones that have been the hardest to learn. Being a parent is, at times, nothing of what I thought it would be and at other times everything I did think it would be. I had been a teacher for almost two decades before becoming a mother and thought I would slide into motherhood like a pro. Well, I was more wrong than ever in my thinking. The love that I have for our children is indescribable, immeasurable and overwhelmingly unconditional. With that being said, we have had a wild ride of parenting thus far!! The highs are so high and the lows are so low and the in-betweens are so validating. There is no manual and there are no wrong or right way of doing things. There just is love!

I am so grateful that my husband, Bruce and I are on the same page when it comes to parenting. The biggest lesson that I have learned in this wide ride called life is there is no normal, there is only what is best for our family at the time. The only constant is the fact that nothing stays the same and change is inevitable, so I am enjoying the ride!

List Items, or places that mark special gratitude for the ones I love

The one item that comes to mind that holds special place in my heart is my mother's wedding ring. I believe my father chose this ring because he loved flowers. My mother's wedding ring's diamonds remind me of a daisy; his favorite flower. There is a round diamond in the center surrounded by a ring of mini diamonds that could represent the petals. This style is actually popular right now which does warm my heart. I think this style is so timeless.

The reason why my mother's ring is so special to me is because it represents her. She always wore it, never took it off and it has her essence all over it. When my husband, Bruce asked me to marry him, I told him that that was the ring that I wanted to represent our union of love. My parents loved each other so very much. They were a team, they had their ups and downs, but in the end, they truly wanted the best for each other, and it showed. Unfortunately, their lives here on Earth were short, but their love for each other was everlasting.

I am so proud to say that our love and union continues to be represented in our own marriage through the symbol of my parents love and devotion to each other through my mother's wedding ring. I just love it. It brings me great joy and grounds me in my commitment to my husband and family.

I am so grateful for having parents who really appreciated nature's beauty. One place that I have fond memories of is of a breathtaking park that my mother, father and I would often frequent. It is called Cranbrook House and Gardens located in Bloomfield Hills, Michigan. It is forty acres of natural beauty which includes a tropical oasis and a 1908 English Tudor home you can tour. It was the original home of the property before the land was donated to be used as a Fine Arts Graduate Program School and art museum. The place is absolutely breathtaking. I remember my father sharing his love of flowers with me, especially African violets, azaleas and his favorite; roses. He would comment on all of the different types of "perfumes" each rose emitted and really did take the time to "smell the roses". My mother would love to walk in the "oriental gardens" as she called them and walk over a beautiful arched bridge to a little island oasis in the middle of the garden. We would spend much time there, soaking up nature's healing properties. My father would marvel at the beautiful grass surrounding the beautiful main house overlooking many fountains. He would say to me, "Look at all of the different shades of green, some even have a hue of blue". He was such a romantic.

Since moving back to Chicago in 2000, I have returned to visit the Cranbrook gardens many times. I have brought my family there to share in the fun and to continue the traditions my parents started with me. It is very liberating to me to be able to relive the fun through the eyes of my children. It is still a magical place to explore, dream and absorb nature's life-giving force.

The first time I returned to Cranbrook after moving to Chicago, I was so excited to share with my family my most favorite tree in the world that was part of the Cranbrook grounds. The tree seemed 100s of years old. It was planted over-looking a majestic lake. It had flowing, willowy, low limbs ready for climbing. It was scared with many lovebird's initials, since it was the tradition. It was a great place to have a picnic, or just some place to curl up with a blanket and a good book. It brought me great peace and tranquillity; it was a home away from home to me. I had great memories of it, I had great dreams of my children climbing on its limbs and swinging on its branches, carving their initials for all to see one day.

Though, tragedy struck in 2011. To my horror, the tree, my tree had been struck by lightning and there was caution tape surrounding it due to its unstable nature. We took pictures of it and I shared my many stories about it and said goodbye to it. I thanked it and felt gratitude for the times we did get to share together. We last visited the park in 2019 and my tree was now just a stump, a majestic stump, nonetheless.

The book, The Giving Tree, by: Shel Silverstein came to mind. It is a book about a tree that kept giving and giving to this boy until it had no more to give and finally the only thing it had to give back was a place to sit. I did just that. I sat on her stump and recalled the fond memories that I had with her. It brought a big smile to my face and warmed my heart. We took pictures of us sitting on its stump and it was blissful, magical and healing all over again. I still provided great joy. I took some wood chips home from the tree and now carry them in my car as a reminder of good times gone by. The lesson here; change is inevitable, but if you are accepting of change you will never deprive yourself of joy you have stored in your heart.

Does one have to overcome serious setbacks or challenges to be successful

I wish I could say that I have always given myself unconditional love, support and trust, but that has not been the case. My old self had been really hard on myself. If I failed to live up to my own expectations, I would not be forgiving or supportive of myself. I would become my worst enemy and nothing ever good came out of that. I also allowed other people to treat me with such disrespect. Over the years, this mistreatment of myself and the allowance of others to treat me with disrespect had taken toll on me emotionally and physically to the point where I became physically unwell as I have already stated. The stress and emotional turmoil that I allowed into my being wreaked havoc with my immune system and mental health so much so that I decided to quit my passion of teaching. That was the hardest thing in the world that I have ever done.

My husband was my biggest supporter. He was there unconditionally supporting me, loving me and trusting that quitting was the best thing I could do for myself and my family at that time. He had told me years later that he felt if I had continued the work lifestyle I was living, I would have not been living much longer. I, on the other hand, had a different opinion and was remorseful for quitting. Though now, I do believe that it was the best thing I have ever done for myself and my family. I can't even imagine returning to that lifestyle of living again.

It took two years from 2016-2018 of soul searching, and finding the root cause of my physical problems through doctors, nutritionists, physical trainers, supplements, medications, etc. to regain my health back to a point where I have never felt more better physically, emotionally, mentally and spiritually stronger than ever before. You might call my soul searching, healing time from 2016-2018 my "dark night of the soul" and call this present moment my "awakening" into a new being of unconditional love, support and trust for myself and others. It is a beautiful thing.

Did I have to go to through all that drama to be "awakened", did I have to beat myself up and allow others to also do the same to become successful, liked and loved? NO!! Did I have to have serious setback and challenges to be successful? The answer is NO!!! Did I know any better at the time? Again, the answer was NO!! Do I know better now? Yes, now I do. Was it a long road to get to my answer? Yes. I have always been a great supporter of Oprah. She has a phrase that I often use. It is: "When you know better you do better". I am doing BETTER!! I am doing what I have been meant to do all along.

I am sharing this story to share my vulnerability, to help maybe guide you to a place of your own awakening, and to let you know that you are lovable unconditionally no matter what. You are going to make mistakes and that is okay, think of them as lessons, stopping posts for clarity, because when you know what you don't want, then you know what you do want. Don't take your mistakes, whatever they are, personally and beat yourself up about them. Forget the mistake, remember the lesson. Be your best friend, the friend you have always wanted, needed and longed for. Nothing is more important than how you feel right now, so feel good unconditionally, regardless of the conditions. Learn to please yourself first, love yourself first, have fun with yourself first and see what you attract, become and achieve. Surrender to the flow of life and start LETTING things happen instead of MAKING things happen, it is quite freeing to let go of the controlling oars in your life and take that "boat ride" of surrender by riding that stream down life's ever-winding road. Once you come to a place of peace and calm in your life, watch what unfolds right before your eyes. It will blow you away!! It has for me!!

Right now you are reading a chapter in this book that I was invited to be part of as Team Vicky, which by the way I almost gave up on, because I was chosen to be part of the Top 50 participants in a contest called THE NEXT IMPACTOR!!! Not in a million years did I think I would be granted the opportunity to be participating in such manifestations of greatness. See what happens when you let go of the oars!! Great things, my friend, great things.

I have such gratitude for the unconditional love and support of my husband Bruce, who saw what I could not see. I was blinded from the greatness that was inside me all along. It was just hiding behind all of the muck and yuck of negative self-talk, a closed-mindset and hate. You too have this greatness inside of you, so be the person you were meant to be on this Earth. Let your inner light shine as a beacon of hope for others who have none, for you never know what the creator has in store for you if you never let Him work his magic through you. Be that empty vessel that he can fill with his greatness and watch how your life will be transformed in ways you could never imagine

If I had the power to solve one and only one problem, it would be...

If I had the power to solve one problem in the world, it would be the problem of people feeling lack of love and worthiness for themselves in their lives. Feelings of unworthiness and being unlovable are not who we are at our core, it is just a lie that we say to ourselves that then becomes a negative habit of thinking because of not loving ourselves enough.

I would want to bring hope to those people who feel that life is a hopeless uphill battle, when in reality, one has to love and respect oneself and feel the worthiness inside for their light to shine bright on the outside. Just remove those thoughts that create barriers to the beauty that one possesses from the inside out and one's light will be able to shine bright. I do believe this with all of my heart!!

My favorite author regarding this topic is Brene Brown. She is the expert. In her book, <u>Daring Greatly</u>, she suggests that having the courage to be vulnerable is the key to letting your light shine. She continues to share that being vulnerable involves uncertainty, risks and emotional exposure and brings love, belonging, joy, courage empathy and creativity to the forefront. I believe it is the core to all of our emotions.

As I ponder when I have shown my vulnerability, my thoughts keep migrating to when I was chosen to be one of the Top 50 contenders in the The Next Impactor. The contest chose 50 people who wanted to share their missions with the world to be global impactors. I entered a video sharing my mission of The Gift of Dyslexia. I had never entered a contest such as this, let alone think I would be chosen to be in the Top 50, but I was!! It was very exciting, but also left me very vulnerable. The 50 of us were divided up into groups of ten and each group had a leader. Vicky Omifolaji was our leader. She made us feel worthy and loved so that vulnerability was allowed to be expressed without any judgement. This was truly a gift. With each passing week, our team continued to become stronger and stronger, more united and focused on common goals helping each other along the way. It was a beautiful example of how eleven strong women can come together to be global impactors allowing their vulnerability to be their strength and not their weakness. It was life changing. They will forever be my soul-sisters.

My purpose in life

While cleaning out the attic when I was still living in Michigan in 1998, I came across a piece of homework paper that seemed like it was written when I was in the first grade. The title was: What I Want When I Grow Up. The page was numbered vertically from 1-3. The first mission statement was: I want to be a teacher. The second mission statement was: I want to have two children, a boy and a girl. The third and final statement was: I want to be rich. I don't remember what the assignment was for, or even if it had to be intangible things. I actually don't even remember writing those words. What I do remember is the fact that sentences 1-3 were very accurate mission statements and have come to fruition.

I have always known my mission in life. It is almost as if I knew it in the womb that I was going to teach. Family members and close family friends remember me playing "school" with my stuffed animals at a very young age. They would tell me that I would line them up, create a classroom full of students and be their teacher. My childhood friends remember me always having to be teacher when we played school too. It really has been a blessing and a no brainer when it came to knowing what I wanted to be when I grew up. In 1991, I accomplished mission # 1. I became an elementary teacher.

My second mission was to have a little boy and a little girl. In 2005, I delivered a healthy baby boy name Michael Paul and in 2007, I delivered a healthy baby girl named Eliana Pina. I believe becoming a mother is by far the greatest mission there is on this Earth. One creates a being of pure, positive energy, plants the seeds of growth and then watches this being grow his/her talents into his/her God given mission; and the cycle never ends. If we really stop to think of it, we come to this Earth to fulfill our missions if we are brave enough to embrace it and let our light shine, we will succeed.

Then, who would have thought that in having my daughter, she would facilitate me in combining my mission #1 of being a teacher with mission #2 of being a mother in ways I would have never dreamed about. My daughter Eliana was born with the gift of dyslexia. Once she was diagnosed in Kindergarten in 2011, our whole world changed. This is when my mission #1 of being a teacher and my mission #2 of being a mother merged. When I delivered Eliana, I had already been teaching elementary students for 18 years. I was considered a veteran teacher and thought what more was there to learn about being a teacher that I did not already know, right!!?? Well, God always has a better plan than we ever could dream up on our own, doesn't he??!! As soon as she was diagnosed, I immersed myself into the world of dyslexia. Our children's school district worked very closely with me and we became an alliance, co-teaching my daughter to the best of both our abilities. It was a magical time of learning, trying and succeeding. After I figured out some of the ins and outs of the dyslexic mind, it occurred to me that dyslexia is not a disability, it is just a different way of thinking. Most schools don't know, nor want to know how to teach dyslexic students and would rather call them disabled and ignore the research based, tested programs that help support dyslexic learners. It is such a tragedy and I am here today to uncover this to the world. This is my mission: to spread the news that dyslexia is a GIFT not a disability. I am also here to share the many different ways in which to teach dyslexic students, which is not hard to accomplish. As a matter of fact, the same strategies work for the regular education population just as well. Schools are slow to change and as a result we have students who are told they are dumb and lazy when those statements are the complete opposite of what the truth really is. Children with dyslexia work generally five times harder to process and retain the information due poor instruction that does not support the dyslexic brain functions. An estimated 20% of the population has these gifted brains and the majority of them are either never diagnosed or labeled disabled. This greatly affects their self-esteem which creates a snowball effect that is detrimental to being motivated to learn. If taught using a systematic, sequential, multisensory approach to learning, children who have dyslexia can be taught, can be successful and as a result have a positive self-image of themselves. They will in turn become successful and productive members of our society. In fact, many geniuses have been diagnosed to have dyslexia such as Albert Einstein, Alexander Graham Bell, Thomas Edison, Walt Disney and Steve Jobs to name a few. Dyslexia is genetic and runs in families. The negative stigma surrounding the "disability" cripples the family's self-esteem and most families would rather blame the schools and the teachers for doing a bad job in teaching their children instead of getting to the root cause of the problem and start demanding early intervention testing specifically for dyslexia. Other issues may or may not be present along with the dyslexia diagnoses, such as having ADHD, anxiety, depression, executive functioning issues, sensory issues, to name a few and then the child is misdiagnosed or under diagnosed, so then the root problem is never addressed. This philosophy of thinking leads the child in a downward spiral of failure both academically and emotionally unless interventions are in place. It is a tragedy that can be remediated if the right programs are put in place in the schools before the age of five!! Though some school districts are more dyslexia friendly than others, presently there is a huge home-schooling movement for precisely this reason as schools are slow to change, and parents are not waiting around anymore. GO PARENTS!! BE THE CHANGE!!

In regards to my mission #3 that I wrote on my paper in first grade - to be rich; that's the easiest one of them all. I am rich with love, with faith, family and friends who support me on my mission. Thank you, Eliana, for being my sweet-hearted, compassionate catalyst for change and for helping spread the truth about the Gift of Dyslexia! Thank you to Michael for your creative ways, your kindness and for always supporting the family and thank you to my soulmate, Bruce; my rock, my life, my love and my best friend.

Chapter 7

Noelle Agape

Team Vicky. Noelle Agape and The Journey to the Next Impactor.
Noelle Agape
Noelle Agape MA PPS
NLP Health and Wellness
Counselor
TV Host of The Infinite Wellness Show
International Speaker
NLP and Energy Medicine Trainer
Wellness Retreat Host

"To the Girl who was afraid to speak, know that your voice will change the lives of millions."

My Name is Noelle Agape, I have been a Counselor for the past 17 years with a focus on Health and Wellness. I have 12 years of formal Education and Training in

Psychology, Quantum Physics, Energy Healing, Neuro Linguistic Programing and Yoga.

I am a TV Host of the Infinite Wellness Show and an International Speaker, I've developed and implemented wellness retreats around the world. I've also implemented wellness programs in schools, local Gyms/Yoga Studios and Corporations. My goal is to help clients find balance in their lives so they can live the highest version of themselves. Coaching them to self-mastery; mastering their mind, mastering their ego, mastering their body, mastering their energy and mastering their soul's purpose. My practice is about connecting Mind, Body, Soul and Spirit to Live Your Best Life.

My words to my younger self are, "To the Girl who was afraid to speak, know that your voice will change the lives of millions." The meaning behind it, is that at six years old I was sexually abused by my 13-year-old neighbor for a year. He was my mother's best friend's son and was in my home almost every day of my childhood. I never said a word about the abuse until I was an adult, after being a Counselor. Being sexually abused at six, losing my Grandfather - my Hero - at 15 and dealing with my dad being an alcoholic and abusive to my mother affected me. My father died when I was 21.

The abuse I witnessed him inflicting on my mother affected my life and I developed a pattern of me being with men that were either abusive, an alcoholic or both. It left me feeling unlovable, not worthy and often accepting disrespect. However, since my divorce I have stepped into my purpose of Healing and using my voice as a Beautiful Gift, instead of hiding behind the shame. We are all brought together for an Amazing Purpose. Our pain becomes our Strength, which becomes our Gifts to the world if we face them.

As a little girl, my grandfather was my hero. In my eyes, he was the greatest man on this planet. When I turned 15, I watched him everyday melt from this beautiful, powerful man to a man that was 65 pounds and dying of cancer. Shortly after his death, I felt in my soul that I needed to make an impact on this world. So, I decided to study Psychology in college, but a few months after my twenty-first birthday, my father died of a heart attack. After yet another heartbreaking death, I knew my calling was to help people heal from trauma.

Fast forward to ten years later and already practicing as a Counselor, I was once hit with the harrowing news that my mother was diagnosed with cancer. At this point, I knew I had enough, and that my family was never going to go through this again. I made a conscious choice to move in the direction of Health and Wellness. I learned and put all my knowledge into my mother's recovery. We put her on an alkaline diet of raw natural foods, got her exercising daily, and removed all the limiting beliefs and toxins from her body. With all these changes in practice, I can gladly say that today my mother is ten years cancer free! From the moment my mother was diagnosed, I knew it was my purpose to give people an awareness of wellness. I started on a spiritual journey and learned about connecting the mind, body, soul and spirit to achieve overall wellness.

On top of my graduate degrees in Counseling, Psychology, and Leadership, I also studied Nutrition, Quantum Physics, Energy Healing, Neuro-Linguistic Programing, and Yoga. A combination of the education I acquired helps me in my work, my purpose. Counselling and psychology have developed my understanding of how the brain works and how it thrives, making it possible for me to help my clients remove limiting beliefs stored in their subconscious as children. Studying Neuro-Linguistic Programming and learning how to reprogram the brain, helps me help my clients to change their thought patterns. Quantum Healing and Physics have both developed my knowledge and ability on how to help people align to their highest self. Being an athlete my entire life and through my yoga practice for the past fifteen years, I've learned how nutrition and exercise affect the kinesiology of the brain. Knowing that teaching people to heal their bodies and minds from the inside out was literally my purpose in life. Today, I am living my dream as a TV Host of The Infinite Wellness Show, a Health and Wellness Counselor, International Motivational Speaker and running Wellness Retreats all over the world. I am giving back while guiding people to become the highest versions of themselves, achieving self-mastery and discovering their soul's purpose.

My childhood was so special to me. Although there was massive trauma, I always found the beautiful light in this world. My mother was helped by grandparents to raise me, and I grew up on a resort. I have so many incredible memories from growing up there; so much love and laughter between my family and me. There was one night that was probably the most special of my life. Every Saturday night the resort hosted a "Family Entertainment Night". The song "Brown Eyed Girl" came on and my grandfather, grabbed my hand and swept me onto the dance floor. As I danced on his feet, literally because I was too small, I remember looking up at him as the light shined down on his beautiful bald head. He looked into my eyes and swept me in his arms and sang the song looking right into my eyes. I don't think there has ever been a moment in my life where I felt as much love as I did while he was twirling me, laughing and singing that magical song. In that moment I felt the world disappeared and it was just me and him and nothing else matters. As we were embraced in the magical moment he whispered in my ear, 'Always remember you are a Star. Women should be put on pedestals. Know that you are a princess now, yet one day you will be a Queen'. Today I look back on the dance with my grandfather and know that because of him I stand in all that I am.

Like everyone, my journey has not always been easy. I have dealt with many twists, turns, and obstacles climbing that elusive mountain; starting with abuse, then death twice, then cancer. Little did I know that all of these life-changing events would only be the beginning of the climb. Becoming an entrepreneur and leaving the safety net of a high paying secure job, I literally had to face every single fear I have ever had. In some ways, I knew the trauma my family had endured gave me power. Power to conquer every fear, knowing that fear was just a limiting belief that could be overcome. Eventually, I used that same fear as a motivator and what was once debilitating became empowering, allowing me to know my inner strength. My advice to my clients, as well as every person out there, is to know your strength and power. It all lies within us; we just need to tap into that internal power. Self-mastery comes from within, never from an external source. There will always be obstacles, we just need to have enough Self-Love and Self-Confidence to know we can move them.

My family and friends have been my backbone from day one. Without the support of my "Tribe" of like-minded individuals I would never be where I am today, nor would I be able to make the impact that I do. The support I have from my family, friends, mentors and colleagues has literally been such a huge part of who I am today. Without them, I do not know how I would have gotten through all of the dark moments of my life. We are all in this together. There are moments in life that your role is the supporter and moments in life when you need to put your ego aside and ask for help. None of this is possible without collective consciousness. We all come together to make this entire planet a better place. That's just how it works. It is why we are here. There are always so many negative things that we could focus on. However, I always choose to live my life in gratitude. There is so much in my life I am grateful for. My children are ALWAYS "My Why". They are my angels and always bring me back to who I am at my core.

I am working in my dream job giving back and traveling the world. There are so many moments in my life that have been a catalyst to the next level of my life and I can't say there's one defining moment because there is so many times in life that I can look back and say this was one of the most grateful moments of my life. The birth of my children, owning a company and becoming an entrepreneur, making a global impact, every one of them gave me the opportunity to live in gratitude. If we stop and see that there are always special moments, and if we take each day, knowing that day is a gift and that we are here on this planet to bring the world to a better place, that is when life becomes magical.

I think that we are always learning and always growing. If we stop learning, we stop expanding. I would love to move completely into being a Humanitarian helping spread health wellness and consciousness globally to underrepresented countries. What I would do differently in my life, on a higher level would be to make a Global Impact, stepping into my power and using my gifts globally to help others in need.

If we start to look at things from the collective, as opposed to the individuals, moving from me to WE that's when the shift happens. What many do not understand is we get a choice in our lives. We may not be able to control the circumstances, yet we can always control how we react to them and how we live our life. We get to choose if we want to live in the victim or the victorious life. To me wellness is not just about eating healthy. Overall wellness is connecting the mind, body, soul and spirit and truly living your best life and every day we get to choose if we want to connect with that. My purpose in Life is to help other to live their best life, globally.

When you stand in your power and in your authenticity truly living as you and in your soul's purpose, that is when you're living a successful life. Success doesn't come from an external source; it only comes from within. The same if true for happiness. Looking within to define true happiness and finding it, you are able to bring it out to the world and that's when you actually have mastered your energy, mastered your mind, body, soul and Spirit. Living in self-mastery allows you to bring your gifts to the world and "live your best life".

So how do you get there? You understand the key components to connecting Mind, Body, Soul and Spirit.

Making the Mind-Body connection is the most important part of our overall wellness. When you are disconnected to either the Mind or the Body, your life is out of balance and it shows you that you're disconnected in some way. It shows up as discord, anxiety, anger, frustration, hurt, fear, and sadness. There are five different components to overall wellness The Mind, The Body, The Energy Fields, The Soul, and The Spirit. When all are connected, you live your life in the flow and in perfect alignment. Your body is a beautiful machine, it's intelligent if we listen, it speaks to us. When we remove toxicity from our lives, toxic foods, toxic thoughts, toxic energy, and toxic relationships that is when we move into a state of flow. We must do the internal work before we can have a Mind-Body connection. If the inner work is not done, your life will show you that you are out of alignment in every way.

The Body

The first of the five components is the body. A huge part of this connection is Nutrition. What you put into your body is a direct connection to what comes out of your body. If you are consuming toxic or processed it will not run at its optimum functional level. If the body is out of balance, it shows up as stress, discord, pain, and disease. Fitness is the second component to the body being connected. Know that movement is a key connection to overall health and well-being. When you exercise, it causes neurotransmitters in your brain to fire. It is literally like taking a shot of dopamine. The oxytocin and serotonin that goes to your brain when you actually move your body allows you to think clearly and connects your mind and your body, allowing you to be in alignment.

The Mind

The next, and one of the most important components to overall health and wellness, is emotional health. This encompasses dealing with and working on the limiting beliefs that are stopping you from becoming the highest version of you. Moving past your limiting beliefs and gaining an understanding of why they are there is the key to living out your highest purpose and truly experiencing this life in love, happiness, abundance, and joy. Connecting all the components of well-being allows you to live a life of abundance and freedom. Ego rests deep within your subconscious mind. The ego is connected to our inner child and many times running off old out-dated programs and beliefs that were developed from the age of 0 to 10 years old. False core beliefs will often block us from moving forward in any area of our lives: fear usually being the biggest obstacle that is stopping us from progressing. What we don't understand about fear is that it is always there to teach us and help us move to the highest version of ourselves. We must do the internal work before we can have true a Mind-Body connection.

The Energy Fields

Everything is energy. With that said, our entire make-up is made of energy. The Human energy system consists of different levels of vibrations and frequencies. What most don't know, is that everything exists in the energetic fields before it manifests into our so-called reality. There are many different vibrational levels of the quantum field Chakras are energy systems in our body where we store our emotions and psychological beliefs as energy. The chakra system starts at the crown of our head moving through our body to the base of our spine. The chakra system is where we store our energy in our body and our emotions are stored on an energetic level. When the chakra system is blocked, every area of our life gets stuck and it shows up as lack, anxiety, depression, sickness, disease and so much more. A well-aligned energy system promotes health, vitality and well-being. When the chakra system is flowing well all systems in the body are energetically nourished and the immune system is enhanced. A person feels grounded and in complete balance with who they are. However, old stagnant energy, or imbalances can occur within these chakras, and the energy fields. This is due to past traumas which can be physical, physiological, or emotional in nature. They show up in our body as a state of disease. When your chakras are balanced, you live your life in perfect harmony, flow, and alignment.

The Soul and Spirit The final stage of overall Wellness is connecting to your soul's purpose. Each of us have come here for two reasons, to experience this journey and expand to a higher version of ourselves. We all have what I call an internal GPS system. It is our connection to God, source, the universe and our highest self. This GPS is our connection to our soul and its purpose; it is constantly guiding us in the direction of expansion. Life teaches us lessons all day, every day, to guide us towards that expansion. It will teach us the same lesson over and over again with different places and different people until we embody the lesson completely. When you are disconnected from your soul and your life's purpose, it shows up in your life as chaos, anxiety, depression, and disease. When you're not living your highest truth, it shows up as lack, anger, discord, sadness, fear, guilt, and shame. When you live your life at higher vibrational energies such as love, joy, happiness, and peace, you are connected to your highest self and moving toward expansion. When you are connected to your soul's purpose and you are truly "LIVING your best life", you embody a healthy body, a healthy mind, healthy soul, and a healthy spirit while living in a beautiful flow of alignment. This is when you have an 'incredible dance' with the universe.

If I had the power to solve one and only one problem in the world, it would be to move the vibration of the planet from hate, anger and lack; to love, peace, joy and abundance. This is when we truly change the world. When we realize that the emotions are just there to teach us and that they are our life lessons, the shifts in our lives will happen. When we understand that emotions are a tool for teaching us and guiding us to our higher self, we develop self-mastery in this life.

I believe that your thoughts become habits, and habits become beliefs, then beliefs become your reality. I Truly believe we create our own reality and our outer world always matches our inner world. If your reality is not what you want, it is because you have limiting beliefs from your childhood experiences that are stored in your subconscious mind that are blocking you from living your best life. I am a licensed counsellor and an NLP Master Trainer, so I work with the subconscious on a daily basis. Working with the subconscious I understand that beliefs are truly more powerful than we even realize, they truly create one's outer reality. When you understand what limiting beliefs are and how you can overcome them and remove the blocks in your life, that is when you can move to truly standing in that power and creating the life of our dreams.

So, what exactly is a limiting belief?

A limiting belief is a belief or block that was formed in your childhood from the age from 0 to 10. During those ages, your brain is like a sponge and it absorbs anything that is put into it. This is when the core of your beliefs is formed. They are stored in your subconscious and are also stored in your body as energy. So, the first limiting belief is I'm not worthy. I am not worthy/ deserving emanates out into your world as lack. Lack of love, money, support and physically manifests as weight gain or illness. The second is I'm not good enough. This emanates out into the world as many failures in life or trying to make things happen and they never come to fruition. Physically, this manifest often as being abused or lack of boundaries. Often people feel taken advantage of or sit in the place of victimhood when they are carrying the I am not good enough block. This can also physically lead to being sick, frequent pain and disease. The third limiting belief is I'm not lovable. This emanates in your life as bad communication or connection with people and often leads to many heart breaks. Sometimes people just disconnect completely because they feel they are not lovable enough for others, so it is easier to disconnect from the world. Physically, lack of selflove leads to eating disorders, abuse or addiction. It could also lead to self-harm in many different forms as well as self-sabotage in many areas of your life. The fourth limiting belief is I'm not safe secure or protected. This often shows up as stress, anxiety and fear. Many times, something happened in your childhood that caused you to not feel safe, secure or protected. Financially, money will be blocked in your life or it will come in and go very quickly. With this limiting belief, often life's a struggle for survival and you are in fight or flight mode. Nothing comes easily and if it does it manifests as pressure or a tremendous amount of stress. Again, physically it manifests as abuse, lack of boundaries, fear, worry, anxiety, nervousness, panic attacks, disease and self-harm. The last limiting belief is I am not whole or complete. This emanates as lack in every area of your life. Always longing for something more, never being satisfied or content with what you have. This is often connected to sadness, depression, envy, and jealousy, many people who carry this belief feel they can't break free from their past and cannot enjoy even the smallest gifts in life nor can they live in the present moment. Physically, this manifests as depression, sadness, low self-esteem, not having body awareness or disconnected from their body completely, many live in victimhood, and are looking for happiness from an external source as opposed to finding peace and happiness within themselves. Many times, this leads to addiction, being taken advantage of, clinging on to toxic relationships and things, co-dependency and fear of loss.

Having these beliefs stored in your body as emotions come through into your reality. Many say your thoughts become your reality, the truth is your thoughts become habits and habits become beliefs and then your beliefs become reality. So, if you believe that you're not worthy then that emanates into the world your value or your worth and that is exactly what your world will show you. The truth is that these limiting beliefs are just here to teach us. Push us to just to be the best version of ourselves because none of this is true. Our truth is we are SO worthy, lovable, good enough, safe and complete. It's just our hurt inner child that absorbed a belief when we were little and have held onto something that is not true.

Behind the limiting beliefs are five core emotions that are always attached to the false core beliefs. The first emotion is FEAR; and anytime you fear something it is really living in the future. You are not living in the present nor having gratitude for what you already have in this life. The second is ANGER; and when you have anger towards somebody it's really just anger within yourself. This anger is just showing you that it is something that you need to work on with you. So if somebody really makes you angry it's something that you need to work on within you. Working on yourself will push you to be the best version of yourself. The third core emotion is SADNESS. Sadness or depression is really just having an attachment to the past and not living in the present moment. In order to release sadness, you need to look at what you are holding onto from your past that you need to release. The sadness is teaching you it is time to let go and move to a better place of growth. The fourth core emotions are GUILT and SHAME. When you have guilt and shame, it's connecting you to something that you are not feeling worthy of. So the guilt and shame is there to teach you about something within you and to correct what went wrong. Forgiveness is the key to healing here. The last core emotion is HURT and hurt is basically the same as living in the past. It is the same as fear because it's not letting go or releasing some pain that you stored in your body. The way to release hurt is also through forgiveness. Forgiven heals you and removes you from the victim mentality. Forgiveness of the situation forgiveness of yourself and the ultimate healing, is forgiving the person that hurt you.

What many of us don't know is that we have Emotional Set Points and Emotional Triggers. These triggers are actually there to teach us of the inner work that we have to do. Emotional set points are boundaries that need to be pushed passed to promote our growth. Once we learn the lesson that we are supposed to be taught, they are released. Almost all of our set points were created at some point in our lives, most of them through our childhood. Emotional set points will come up in your life with different people or different circumstances until you learn the lesson and move past them. Something will come up in your life where you will have growth and then for some reason you will fall back or many times the growth or the movement will not happen at all; this will be a hundred percent because of your emotional set points. The set points are always fear-based. If you stop and look at the patterns in your life that keeps repeating themselves with different people and different circumstances, the lesson will be there for you to release the set point. You define emotional set points by the patterns that have been repeating in your life as well as the triggers. If someone, or something triggers you to have an emotional reaction and it's been a pattern in your life, follow the pattern back and connect it to a False Core Limiting belief; and that is where your emotional set point is. Emotional triggers are connected to false core beliefs from when we were children.

The beliefs that we spoke of above, I'm not worthy, I'm not good enough, I'm not safe secure and protected, or I'm not whole and complete; none of this is true. I want you to stop for a minute and find something that really bothers and annoys you frequently. It's connected to a pattern that's been in your life and that's where your trigger is. If you want to break the pattern and remove the trigger ask yourself these questions… At what age did I develop this trigger and why? What is the trigger trying to teach me? What is it going to take for me to break through this pattern? Then take action where needed, to move forward with releasing the trigger and the pattern.

It is my belief that self-love is the most important part of overall health and well-being. Everything that is going on in your world comes down to how much self-care and self-love you are giving yourself, also how much you are allowing to receive in your life. Many times, we block our greatness, our abundance, our love, or even our health, because we do not feel deserving, worthy, lovable or safe enough to allow it into our lives because we don't have love for ourselves. Self-love and self-care is the key to everything you're longing for in your life. Look inside yourself and see where you are not giving yourself enough self-love. Where are you not seeing the magnificence that is within you? Where are you not living your purpose? Where can you care for yourself more? Are you taking care of everyone else and not taking care of you? Is your cup filled so much that it's overflowing and then you can't help others? Everything comes back to how can you love yourself more in every area of your life. If there is a place in your life that there is lack, look inside and see where you're not having self-love in that area. I promise you, the more you focus on self-love, the more abundance, love and support will show up in your life. You will have more love, happiness, joy, laughter and a life of fulfilment. Everything, absolutely everything, comes down to self-care and self-love. Invest in YOU, it is the greatest investment you will ever make.

Life teaches us if we listen. It shows us the way and guides us on our path to our higher self. Often times, we are not willing to listen. Life lessons are not always fun and often throw a massive wrench into what we believe is our reality. God, the universe, source, shows us over and over again how to go towards our higher selves. When we don't listen to that, the biggest lesson come in. Each of us has a unique blueprint when we are born. We each of us, have a specific gift and a purpose to contribute to the expansion of humanity. The answer is always there, we just need to listen.

Growth spurts are periods in life when your soul is ready to expand, except your subconscious is not ready to move on and wants to stay safe or has a fear of change. It is when the energy is stagnant, and you haven't moved through the life lessons. Every time you move to the next stage of your life, often you have to move through a growth spurt. This is when, all of a sudden, life freezes and nothing is moving forward. Growth spurts always happen when you have something energetically that needs to be moved through emotionally so you can grow to the next stage of your life. Often the reason we have not moved to the next level is fear-based because there is something that is scaring us from moving on from our comfort zone. Whether it's I'm not worthy, I'm not deserving, I'm not safe secure and protected, or I'm not lovable; it is always one of these beliefs that hold us back. The number one thing to understand is that we get to choose. We get to choose our growth. We get to choose our time that it takes to move forward. We get to choose to step into our life's purpose. The Universe is always going to show us every option that is out there; good, bad, negative, positive or indifferent. It is going to show us, so we get to choose through the growth spurts in our life and move to the highest version of ourselves.

People sometimes become stagnant in a growth spurt. They become frozen, not knowing what the next step is, because they feel that they've tried and they tried and just can't get through to the next level so they give up and they go back to their comfort zone. Often, they give up right before the breakthrough. Yet I promise you; if you face your fears and learn the life lesson, get through the process, it's so much more beautiful on the other side. That is where your purpose and the magic is waiting for you.

Receiving love

For some people, it's very easy to give love to others; yet often times it's hard to receive love. When this is the case, people often push love, abundance and happiness away. Receiving love is directly correlated with how much self-love you have for yourself. This mostly is a direct correlation of how you were raised and how open your heart is. People were often never taught how to receive love because their parents did not show them love, so they have a hard time receiving anything good in their life. They may have been hurt in the past or are closed off from a broken heart. The hurt case them to block off their heart from receiving what whatever it is they may want in their life. So often times when you have abundance blocks, it's very much connected to self-love. Your past experiences show up in anyway in your life that you have blocked yourself off from receiving love.

Some people develop heart walls, which are many emotions that are built up together as clusters of energy, closing off your heart space. Your heart space, in your heart center, is the most important direct connection to you receiving in every area of life. If you are disconnected from your heart center, it will show up as being disconnected to people in your life, disconnected to the things you want, and disconnected from your soul's purpose. As humans, emotionally the most important thing is to feel connected and not feel rejected. If we are lacking in either of those two, we will put an emotional wall around our heart. In life, if someone feels rejected or disconnected, often they will push people away on purpose because they don't feel safe enough to let love in. Any disconnection from others is because a person doesn't have enough self-love, so they protect themselves from getting hurt over and over again and remain closed off because that is safer than being hurt again. When you open your heart you receive the magic of love and all of its power, that is when you are connected to your heart center; that you are connected to your higher self.

All this brings me to my journey over the last six months of being in a competition called The Next Impactor. I entered knowing the creator of the competition, Loren Michaels Harris. I knew he was a conscious creator and knew anything he was creating; was something I would love to be a part of as well. What I didn't know was how this journey was going to change my life. As I sat on my bed listening to them announce the people that made it into the Top Fifty Competitors, I remember specifically thinking how great it would be if I was on the team of a few of the coaches that I had previously known. At that moment something came over me and out loud I said, "Ok God I know this is moving me forward to truly LIVE in my purpose, so please put me on the team that is The Greatest and Highest Good For All." At that exact moment I was chosen to be on to Team Vicky, literally within seconds of me saying that. Team Vicky is a team of twelve conscious women. The power we have as a collective is unbelievable.

From day one we were a TEAM and there was never a moment that wavered in that. Never a moment of ego, of selfishness, of being unsupported or unconditionally loved. As I mentioned I have been an athlete my entire life. With that comes a strong sense of competition, Willpower, grit and grind. It puts you in a space of the end result being winning. Within Team Vicky, there was zero space for that. We were a collective and Together WE stand in Love was the Theme. As I grew closer to some of the most amazing women I have met in my life, I opened my heart to truly being present in the competition. I began to engage with ALL of the contestants not just my team. Soon I realized that every person in this competition was an Amazing Human; that as a collective, we were put together to make massive shifts in this world on the global level.

As the competition went along so did the challenges that come from stepping out of my comfort zone. Very quickly I was faced with some massive life challenges. On a personal level I had to move from my home in the middle of the competition, I ended a relationship of almost five years and my business completely shifted from the roles I had been comfortable with to opportunities of incredible exposure. I was no longer safe to live in my old life. Soon I found out that each of us on Team Vicky had gone through intense changes internally as well as externally. It was within that time that I heard that still small voice in my head that whispered, "remember you asked to be placed on a team that was The Greatest and Highest Good for ALL involved." Each and every moment that we were pushed to our limited emotionally, physically and mentally selves, we were supported and loved and encouraged to make it to the other side. Through this entire journey I found love, a deeper love for myself and others that I had no idea was in me. I found a community that I have allowed into my life and my heart. I found how to move from Me to "We" and separate from ego. Yet, most of all I found My Life's Purpose as a Humanitarian and Global Impactor. Through The Next Impactor, I found My Highest Version of Myself. I found how important what I teach truly is. I found a deeper sense of tapping into my soul to step FULLY into my purpose of Global Impact. The Gratitude I have found within Team Vicky and every person in this competition, was more than I could ever imagine or ask for. Collective consciousness at its best. TOGETHER WE ARE THE CHANGE.

Connect With Noelle Agape https://noelleagape.com Facebook https://www.facebook.com/noelleagapelove
Instagram @noelle_agape

Chapter 8

Sharon Ton

Sharon worked for twenty-three years, eighteen of them in Pediatrics. Some of her job roles included Geriatric nursing, Newborn Nursing plus Quality Control, and School Nurse. She also worked as a Case Manager and Director of a Pediatric Home Care Agency. She's retired from nursing and now works a Marketing Executive for a Health and Wellness company. Her focus is educating people on how to improve and/or maintain good health which will add years to their life and life to their years.

Sharon currently resides in Chesterton, Indiana with her husband a retired educator. They have two married sons and two grandchildren. Her newest grandchild was fostered and adopted by her oldest son's family. This is so very special for her being fostered and adopted as well. She knows that their relationship will be very special. Her interests are Health Education, gardening, interior design, spending time with her husband and grandchildren.

She is the current President of the Chesterton Woman's Club and an active member of the Chesterton United Methodist Church. The Co-Opvertising Network has recognized her as an influencer at the community level. She has also been recognized in the Health and Wellness Field as a 20/20 member for Better Choices Better Lives.

Creator of "Joining Hands with Hope" to help eliminate child hunger in her community and beyond.

She is currently in the Top 25 of The Next Impactor.

Challenges and tough times happen to everyone but how do we respond? Do we let them hold us back? Do we feel sorry for ourselves? Do we blame others for what happened? These were responses I had many times throughout my life that I knew were unhealthy. So what should you do? I found later in my life that these times were a part of my purpose and helped me grow. I learned from them and found others who I could help going through the same thing.

My older brother, once we reconnected later in my life, filled in some of my memories. The trauma caused me to block a lot of this extremely difficult time, and I am so grateful that he shared what he remembered. In the beginning, my childhood from birth to the age of six was extremely difficult for my family. My parents and seven children were living in poverty. It was hard as a child, not knowing if I and my siblings would have food each day. As a child, I did not understand why. I just knew we went to bed hungry and got up hungry. I do remember being in a car frequently and taking care of my younger siblings because my mom was pregnant often. Once when we were all in a car, as we passed this big building, I was told that our dad was there. This was confusing because I didn't understand why. Later I found out that the building was a jail. We relied many times on family to help us out and visiting them was a common occurrence. They would bathe, feed us, give us a place to sleep and when we were leaving they would give us money. I felt my mom's role in life was to have babies and my dad's was to support us which he wasn't able to do.

At six years of age, our lives changed dramatically. My dad was in jail for stealing his boss' car. He said he was only borrowing it. His boss didn't see it that way because he took it out of state, which is a felony. This left my mom with seven children, no income and scared as to how she was going to support her family. She had no job skills and no one to watch us even if she did get a job, so we moved into government housing in Hammond, Indiana. Our living conditions went from bad to worse. What was she meant to do now? Reaching out for help was the only way.

We were visited by DCS several times but the living conditions worsened. On the final visit, my siblings and I were loaded into a car with my mom crying "please don't take my children". We were holding each other, crying, terrified and didn't understand what was going to happen to us. My brother and I tried to "keep it together" for the younger ones. What happened was traumatic for all of us. As a mom, this experience had to be painful; to lose all her children with her husband in jail. What a horrific moment!!!

We were each taken to different foster homes. We not only lost our parents but our siblings too. I can't imagine how it was for the younger ones. Why did this happen? I didn't understand. Maybe we were bad and that was why we were removed. The whole experience made me angry, sad and confused. To make things worse, my dad came to visit me several times and told me he planned to come and get me and my brothers and sisters as well, but this never happened. Abandoned again!!!

The foster home was very difficult in many ways. I was asked to watch the other children and was not able to go outside to play in the neighborhood. I was often taken to the principal's office at school for fighting because of bullying. I was very angry and felt there was no way out. I would cry myself to sleep, have nightmares and I had a bed wetting problem. As an adult, I appreciate and want to thank all foster parents for the gift they are giving to many children. You give them security, emotional support, love, food, clothing, and a safe place to live. They are confused, sad, angry and feel abandoned by their family. Foster parents are God's angels.

HOPE presented itself when I was seven. My caseworker came to visit me and told me a family, who had a son and couldn't have any more children, wanted to adopt a girl. They observed me and the caseworker in a Gary ice cream parlor and THEY PICKED ME!!! I was excited yet scared.

They made me feel very special on my first home visit. What a surprise when I entered their home. Here I would never have to worry about food, have a safe permanent home and, would you believe, my own bedroom.

They asked me if I wanted them to adopt me. I said YES YES YES!!! MY new family saved me from child hunger and much more. I was now figuring out who I was in this new family; new parents and an older brother. In the beginning, it was hard to trust because of what I had experienced at a young age. I worried that if I misbehaved they would send me back. My new family gave me unconditional love, earned my trust over the years and helped me blossom to be the woman, mother, and wife I am today. The most defining moment in my life happened at eight years of age when I was officially adopted by this wonderful family. Standing with them in front of the judge in his chamber was a life-changing moment I will never forget. The judge asked if I wanted to be adopted by them and I, of course, said YES!!! I felt safe and secure with my new family. It is hard to put it into the words, given the experiences I had growing up; how much time does the reader have?

At approximately nine years of age a terrible, scary thing happened. My maternal aunt and family would come to visit us from Chicago. They were kind and accepting of me as a part of this new family. This is extremely difficult to share even today! Only my husband and my children know. My older cousin asked me to watch television with him in my parent's upstairs bedroom. He asked me to touch different parts of his body in appropriately. Eventually leading to his male area. I was highly uncomfortable with this request. He said he would give me money if I did. I was afraid but did it. He said that what he made me do was alright, that it was our secret. This happened more than once. I was so afraid that if I told my parents they would be angry and say it was my fault. Would they give me back? Remember, I was very insecure then. Every time I was around him for the rest of my life I was extremely uncomfortable. I avoided time around him as much as I could. In my summertime, at our summer cottage, he did other inappropriate things and he would make sure I saw him. This was a bad thing that happened to me. In order to heal, I tell myself what I would tell any child; I was the victim and he took advantage of me because he knew I was vulnerable. I have let go of it. I'm not going to let his actions control my thoughts.

I have many wonderful childhood memories - playing outside with the neighborhood children, going to our family cottage where we spent all our summers. As soon as school was out, we packed up and went there for the entire summer. The cottage was rustic with no indoor plumbing. There was a pump in the kitchen sink which had to be primed to work. The best water I ever tasted! We took showers in our bathing suits outside since we didn't have a bathtub. We used an outdoor custom built outhouse my dad and uncle built. It was made of brick blocks with two seats. This was not the typical outdoor "John" for sure. My parents even bragged about it! They taught me to swim and fish. My brother and the neighborhood children played outside; badminton, woodfle ball (version of baseball) and a lot of swimming, because there was no television. On rainy days we would play cards and board games. On cool nights, we would have a bonfire and roast hotdogs and marshmallows. My mom tutored me every summer, for many years, because I was delayed emotionally and academically. My parents decided I needed to repeat first grade because of that. She talked to my teachers every year, who gave her things she could do over the summers to help me catch up. This showed me how my parents cared and wanted the best for me. My new brother was so smart and hardly studied getting A's. I was jealous but he was supportive and helped me when I was struggling in school. My maternal Aunt and her family had a cottage next door, we spent a lot of time with them. I missed my school and Gary neighborhood friends, but what an amazing time I had there. Wonderful!!! I have a smile on my face when I think of that time in my life. Both my time at the cottage and at my school and home in Gary were transformative. Everyone was so accepting of me. Many wonderful memories I continue to cherish today.

Growing up, my mom was a "stay at home mom" which was so typical in the 50's. She helped us get ready for school with a good breakfast. Because I was only three blocks from school, I went home for lunch every day. I would ask periodically to eat lunch at school with some of my friends, which she'd agree to. That was the life they wanted for me too - get married, have children and be home for them. Going to college wasn't necessary for women. In high school, I didn't take the necessary college prep courses even though my counselors kept telling my parents that I had so much potential. My counselors continued to encourage them to let me take college prep classes, but that didn't happen. It was different for my brother, who they expected to go to college. He received a full football scholarship to Princeton University. He didn't apply himself and so lost his scholarship. He was drafted into the Army and when discharged, came home with his wife, and worked at US Steel where our dad worked. So sad because I would have loved to have such an opportunity.

After I was married, I shared with my husband that I would love to be a nurse. At the time we had a five year old son and I was a "stay at home mom". With his encouragement, I started night school for classes needed to get into a good college. I applied to Purdue University's nursing program and was accepted. I was so excited. However, due to raising our son, I decided to take pre-nursing classes part time. I enjoyed being home with him. I enrolled in nursing classes and found out that I was pregnant with baby number two. It was a family decision to stay home for the first year of his life. I treasured that time with him. When the year passed, I was able to start my nursing classes and my younger son was with a babysitter only when I was taking classes. The older one was in elementary school. Seven years later, I received my nursing degree and passed my RN state boards. I love children and so I decided to work in the pediatric field. Of my twenty three year nursing career, eighteen were working with children. I recently realized that my love of children may be because of the absence of my birth siblings. My husband and I strongly encouraged our sons to go to college. They both graduated from Purdue University with Technology Engineering Degrees.

Over the years, I always wondered what happened to my birth parents and siblings and thought of them often. Could I find them? Would they want to meet me? Would my adoptive parents understand why I wanted to search for them? I didn't want them to think I didn't love them. When my youngest son was about three, I decided to find my birth family. I was scared as to what I would find. Were my siblings alright? What happened to my birth parents? After a long search, I found my siblings, my father, and extended family members. I found I had fifteen siblings. WOW!!! After we were removed from our mother, they got back together and had three more children. My mom died at 32 of cervical cancer so I was never able to get to know her. This was difficult to deal with because I had lost my memories of her. I am not sure why; too painful? After my mom died, my dad remarried and gained a stepdaughter and him and his wife had four more children.

The first time I met my birth father was awkward and shocking. My husband and my two children were with me, thank goodness. He lived in a dilapidated and not very clean small house with his stepdaughter. What I saw was a small man sitting in a chair, oxygen on, and dark discolored feet. I found out that his health was very poor: heart disease, diabetes and emphysema. I don't know why, but in my early life I had put him on a pedestal. It was eye-opening, shocking and not what I expected. I guess I didn't know what to expect. I saw pictures of naked girls on a wall, which I didn't let my children see. He talked about how he tried to find us and losing us was not his fault. I heard that over and over for many years. I found out from his brother that wasn't the case. His brother, who also lived in Southern Illinois, told me that after we were removed, my dad came crying to him about his children being taken away, asking what he should do. He told his brother there was a court hearing in Gary soon for him and my mother to try to get us back. When my uncle asked why he was there with him in southern Illinois he couldn't explain. My uncle told him to go back and fight for his children. Sadly, when he got back to Gary the court hearing was over and it was too late.

During the years that followed, I was able to get to know my dad better. I have forgiven him. Learning his story explained a lot of why we lived the way we did. He was never taught or learned how to be a father. At fifteen, he was on the streets with no guidance or direction. It was a true breakthrough to find out the whole story. Finding all my siblings was wonderful. They shared with me their lives and their new families. Most had good experiences, a few didn't. I learned that two of them were adopted by the same family. Two of my brothers went to the same church and school. The adoptive parents agreed to not let them know they were related. The youngest of the seven, was very malnourished and her adoptive parents were told she may not make it. Thank goodness her adopted mom was a nurse. She survived with loving care. Our first reunion was awesome, getting to know each other and my paternal family was terrific. Our birth family treated us as if we were never gone. They shared that if they knew the whole situation they would have given us all homes. I found out that our mom was buried in a pauper's grave. It was so sad when one of my sisters and two brothers went to her grave site. She only had a marker and no head stone. We decided to buy her a headstone with all of her children's names on the back. She deserved more than that. What a wonderful day going to the cemetery and see it in place.

Over the years, my siblings have remained a huge part of my life. I treasure many handwritten letters from them and my father. Four of my siblings have passed but I treasure their memory. This whole experience has been a time for healing, closure and knowing my birth parents loved all of us. They just couldn't financially take care of our family. I also realized how much I love my adoptive family. Finding my family wasn't going to make me love them less, just the opposite. I loved them more because they gave me an amazing life. Words can't express what they meant to me. My story is one of Hope, Healing, Love, and Survival.

I am a member of the Co-Opvertising Network of Entrepreneurs who are doing a peanut butter drive for the NWI Food Bank and Northern Illinois Food Bank. Their goal is to help to feed hungry children and their families. It is shocking how many children live with food insecurities. One out of seven in NWI and two out eight in the United States, live in these circumstances. This is sad since we live in one of the richest countries in the world!! After taking a tour of the food bank, God helped me to see that living and surviving child hunger is why I am passionate to help in any way I can. I know what the challenges and struggles of today's children and families are. This is why I created "Joining Hands with Hope". Many people want to help but aren't sure how, they can be a part of the cause and truly make a difference. When many join hands, we can truly change the world of hunger. I am excited to work with the NWI Food Bank and learn what resources are available. How can "Joining Hands with Hope" help them and also help our community? Food is one of the basic survival needs. Air, water, food and a safe place to live are all important to our survival. There is much more to provide besides food. It is important to focus on all the issues that lead people to live in hunger. I call them the "six pillars of hunger". They are emotional support, jobs, housing, education, health and finance. There may be more, but that was what I experienced with my family. I will welcome people to join hands with me and the NWI Food Bank. Together we can truly change the world for the better.

In my lifetime, I learned a great deal. I believe that all the struggles and challenges I lived through in my life led me to my purpose with God's help. Learning and growing in difficult times is a challenge but important. When I played the "poor me" card, it was bad for my health; I did this many times. "I believe that my life is my purpose and my purpose is my life". What does one do with the difficult times in life? Do you let them hold you back or reach out to others to help them? As a survivor of child hunger, I decided that I want to help others by sharing my story. Hopefully others see there is hope, healing, love, and power to change. I am blessed, and helping the less fortunate gives me a stronger purpose. This can be difficult when you don't agree with other's beliefs. It is a struggle for me at times. I lean on Jesus' basic message of treating others the way you would want to be treated. This is the way I want to live my life. I have learned to agree to disagree and not judge. We all have the right to our own opinions; some people don't take the time to truly listen to others. We are too busy thinking about ourselves and what we want to say. Listening to each other is vital. "When you're talking you aren't listening." If we haven't walked in their shoes we cannot judge their actions.

I have a good life but is it successful? I believe that success isn't just money and the material things it can buy. Money is necessary to pay our bills, have food on the table. take care of our family and have a place to live. Success to me, is how you treat others you work with, meet through your business and in your community. People need to know that you care and aren't just out for money. I feel I have a good life and am successful because I want to help others as much as I can. You can have a good life and be successful for sure.

I am grateful I entered The Next Impactor Competition in January of 2020. This was a huge defining moment in my life. I was nervous and unsure of whether I had it in me to compete on a global level. I was encouraged by Jeff Levin, co-founder of the Co-opvertising Network of Entrepreneurs to enter the competition. He shared that my mission of child hunger needed to be shared with the world. I saw it as a huge opportunity and I said yes, I need to do this. I am learning how to share my mission of eliminating child hunger in a new way. Being able to go global is scary, but so necessary, because it is a global problem. I discovered ways to reach out and make many connections with people who want to join me on my quest. Doing live Facebook messages, interviewing and supporting other contestants is rewarding. This experience is helping me to get out of my comfort zone. Being in partnership with many impactors and getting to know their missions is a gift. They are truly a gift to all.

Being on Team Vicky and working with a beautiful group of loving, kind, encouraging and supportive women has helped me to work as a team. We each have gifts and talents that we used in all of our challenges. The relationships we made transformed all of our lives. They are my soul sisters and come to this competition with the goal of LOVE. Go Team Vicky!!! if you are asked to do something out of your comfort zone, do it. Follow your God-given message because it will transform your life in ways you could never imagine.

This story is told In Loving Memory of: Birth Parents - Charles and Bonnie Monk, Adopted parents - Walter and Ann Rockwell, and sisters Terry, Sandy, Shawn and brother Mark.

Sharon Ton's CONTACT INFORMATION

HOPE HEALING LOVE AND SURVIVAL

&

BETTER CHOICES BETTER LIVES SECURING YOUR TOMORROW TODAY

&

PILLARS OF HUNGER

Emotional Support, Jobs, Housing, Education, and Finance

For Questions /Information
stonrn@comcast.net

Chapter 9

Elizabeth Schmidt

My name is Elizabeth Schmidt, I was born in Lagos, Nigeria. I am a mother of six lovely adult children, all in their 30s and 40s and they are all doing extremely well in life. I am also a grandmother. A lover of good music, I love to dance. Travelling and nice food are two of my guilty pleasures. I have travelled virtually to all major European countries such as Germany, Spain, United Kingdom and France, just to name a few.

With over 30 years of experience, I am a well-trained retired healthcare professional. In my career I worked with mostly children; supporting them with their mental, social and physical wellbeing. I have a great passion for children's wellbeing; especially those orphaned, underprivileged, abused, raped, homeless and those from poor background. My passion for working with children drove me to establish a free daycare center, nursery and primary school in 1981 called Gracious Kids in Mafoluku Lagos, Nigeria. Gracious Kids is a huge success and many children were able to access education and care, free of charge. These children grew up to be women and men who are doing well today.

In 2002, I established an orphanage called Finger of God Orphanage, which is registered with the Lagos State Government in Nigeria. To the glory of God, the orphanage is still up and running today. I have sponsored, single handedly, more than 20 children on education scholarships. I have empowered many youths with their choice of profession and am still paying and feeding many elderly people in Nigeria. My love and passion for children and the elderly in Africa, is second to none. I am a goal getter and very hard working.

Chapter 10

Emily Seelman

Emily Seelman, co-founder of N4M, brings with her experience in the start-up industry as well as a legal background. She attended Grove City College, a Christian Conservative school located in Grove City, Pennsylvania, where she received her Bachelor of Science degree in Business Marketing; graduating with high honors in Marketing Management and made the Dean's List with Distinction. Her most distinguished honor was being elected sorority president.

After college, Emily attended Duquesne University School of Law and graduated Cum Laude with an award for the highest grade in Expert Evidence. During her time in law school, Emily was an Associate Editor for the Duquesne Law Review Journal and received the Distinguished Junior Staff Editor Award. She served as the law school representative for the Pennsylvania Bar Association and Allegheny County Bar Association-Women in Law Division. She was also Vice President of the Christian Legal Society and worked as a student-representative for the Barbri Bar Preparation Company. She was a three-year Merit Scholarship recipient for high levels of achievement.

Upon passing the bar exam, Emily practiced as an Associate Attorney in the Civil Litigation and Employment law sections of Leech Tishman Fuscaldo & Lampl, LLC, the 13th largest law firm in the City of Pittsburgh. She also worked with the firm's legal cannabis team, preparing applications for individuals applying for Pennsylvania medical marijuana permits.

In 2017, Emily attended Tony Robbins' Unleash the Power Within and Date with Destiny events and realized her passion to live a life of entrepreneurship and to blend work, fun, personal-growth, and service together. She left the "big law firm life" and currently owns and operates a number of start-ups, including TwinMinds, LLC, which operates IEPPal education platform, and Tetra Growth Solutions, a cannabis application and consulting firm. She sits on the Advisory Board for Steel City Hero

Hunts, a nonprofit charity that provides fully funded therapeutic trips to the great outdoors for Pittsburgh veterans. She recently moved from Pittsburgh, Pennsylvania to Charleston, South Carolina to launch a social media platform with her twin, Allison Ferrante. Emily is currently training to compete in her first bodybuilding bikini competition in summer 2019 and she documents the journey on their shared Instagram and YouTube accounts: Emily.and.Allison. She also hosts a YouTube channel called Tetra Growth Systems where she provides basic introductory knowledge of the cannabis space for people who are seeking knowledge but are new to the marijuana industry.

Chapter 11

Sophia Greenstein

I am Sophia Greenstein and I was part of the Next Impactor Challenge to help spread the light of positivity! I try to show everyone that positivity is the way of life! I also try to help people know that positivity is not that hard to see. You can have positivity in your life if you try.

I know that sometimes finding the positive in a bad situation is hard, and that is why I am trying to help people see the positivity in the world! Throughout my entire life, and I am only fourteen years old, I have been through difficult challenges and I have still managed to see the positive light. For example, my sister has a medical issue and she visited many doctors for help. However, instead of taking lots of medication she almost cured herself with diet and exercise! Now, she could have just stayed in the black hole, but she didn't, and she changed her whole life just by a small thing called positivity!

Chapter 12

ALLISON FERRANTE

Allison Ferrante, co-founder of N4M, is a business-owner and full-time mom. She attended her dream school, Grove City College, a college that values both faith and freedom. In the four years she attended college, Allison was the president of her sorority, honor student, named on the Dean's List, was recommended by her peers to be on the homecoming court and received her Bachelor of Science degree in Business Marketing and Management with a focus on Communication Studies. She was immediately hired to work for a prime contractor for the United States Naval Nuclear Propulsion Program (NNPP) after college.

While employed at the NNPP, Allison married the man of her dreams, a United States Marine and now, firefighter. They bought a house, adopted a pit bull and, together, they realized that they had a passion to live a life designed by themselves. They quit their jobs and moved to live by the ocean in sunny Charleston, South Carolina.

Allison competed and placed in her first bodybuilding bikini competition. A year later, they adopted a second pit bull, and she enlisted in the Air Force National Guard. A few months before heading to basic training, Allison found out that she was pregnant with her first child; her sweet, baby boy Micah.

She currently works for the Town of Mount Pleasant full-time, while operating IEPPal, an education platform. She also started a non-profit, Networking4Moms, with co-founder and twin sister, Emily Seelman, designed to provide the resources for stay-at-home moms to be able to re-enter the workforce. Allison also operates a social media platform with her sister called Emily.and.Allison: an Instagram account and a YouTube channel. They are currently in the process of developing a dating App for single parents. She is currently training, post-partum, to compete in her second bodybuilding bikini competition.

Allison has a desire to contribute to her community and improve the lives of those around her by living fully, employing her talents, working hard and loving deeply. Her mission is to uphold the good, the true, and the beautiful, while impacting the world. At the same time, she strives to do the little-noticed disciplines well, like growing in the knowledge of her Creator and raising and training her children in His nurture and Word. She believes in living with deep gratitude and joy.

Conclusion

The women featured in this book are mothers, educators, daughters, grandmothers, sisters, professionals, businesswomen, wives, philanthropists, life changers and so much more. Whatever name they are given, whatever roles they have in their everyday lives, it's important to note that they are all Impactors. All of them have and continue to, contribute to the development of their local communities and society on a whole.

Through their stories, we have witnessed tragedy, struggles, joy, hope, LOVE and most importantly growth. Each woman has grown into the women they are today despite their struggles and challenges. They were all able to not only rise above them but also learn from all the experiences and used it as their motivation to become better versions of themselves. Poverty, addiction, learning difficulties, diseases, and death have affected them in ways some of us can only imagine. However, what is common among all of them is that despite all of this, they have each risen to the occasion by not only improving their own lives but also the lives of many others. To say that they are sources of inspiration isn't enough.

Being an Impactor is about bringing hope and positivity to the world, both of which you have witnessed through the stories shared by these powerful women. Poverty, which is a common concern, has been demonstrated in more ways than one. Firstly, it has profound effects and implications for persons who have and continue to face it. People living in poverty deal with challenges which include lack of access to education and food. Those affected by poverty are often left without their basic needs being met. As a child, Sharon was affected by poverty and faced hunger as a result. Although her birth parents had love for each other and their children, they lacked the resources needed to take care of their family. Sadly, this is something that happens all around the world every day. Children continue to suffer from hunger, homelessness, lack of access to water and many are unable to access education.

The story of Tiuana is one that, unfortunately, many kids and young people can relate to. Although education is a necessity, many people do not have access to it simply because they do not have the financial means. In this book, evidence of people working to eradicate poverty is also present. To enable access to education for people living in impoverished conditions, Elizabeth has built learning facilities in her home country Nigeria. Sharon herself is working to combat child hunger and Beth encourages the world to LOVE each other all in the hopes of helping to eradicate hunger. What these women have all demonstrated is that even with these challenges; hunger, poverty, addiction, death, and self-doubt, change can happen and all it requires is for someone to take that step in the right direction.

Another common factor among all these women is their belief in choice. One has to agree; choice is one of the most important gifts of life. It was quite profound to think of it along the levels that even the Creator who gave that power of choice allows us to make them freely. Given all the adversity they each faced, they could have all chosen to give up, stop pushing, stop wanting and stop believing. Where would they have been? What would their lives be like now? Tiuana could have given up when she couldn't find the $1200 to finish school, Vicky could have told herself she was never going to understand anyway and just gave up on learning altogether and Noelle could have allowed her background of abuse to continue to define her future. Likewise, Barbara after the loss of her second husband could have given up entirely. The greatest thing is that they all made choices and took that first step to become better versions of themselves.

The lesson and importance of support have been laid out for us in so many ways in this book. In essence, having support, someone to encourage you, even if it is yourself is very important. Emily and Allison are working together and supporting each other both in their business and personal life. While many siblings can't sit in the same room spending time with each other, these sisters work together; creating change in the lives of women who also need support and spend additional time training for a competition they will both be entering. Beth is close to her family and just by reading her story we see nothing but a strong support system. The examples are many, somewhere in everyone's life there is a Mr. Anderson, you just have to find him, even if you are your own Mr. Anderson to yourself. It is also important to be supportive and encourage others. Sharon didn't keep the competition to herself. She not only shared it with, but also pushed Barbara to apply, and now they can both share their stories.

What is profound about all these women and Sophia, is the drive and motivation they all have to make the world a better place. The relationship between them is strong enough to overcome any challenge, as they are all intent on achieving the same goal – making a difference. Each person has something different to offer and being a part of The Next Impactor will definitely allow them to freely share ideas worthy of being explored or implemented.

Antonietta's message is one that will be useful in the journey of giving back. Too often the giver forgets that help is also available for them or that it's even possible to take breaks and time for self and the people you love. This often ends with burnout and even medical complications. On your journey to finding yourself and becoming a better you and eventually changing the world, it's important to make time for yourself and take care of your own wellbeing and needs. Aimee's message adds to this as she talks about her journey to learning to care for both her mental health and physical wellbeing. Her message along with that of Noelle's speak about asking for help and accepting support. This is important for someone wanting to or already working to create change: it is important to take care of yourself too.

The ultimate message in this book is that you can achieve anything you put your mind to. You can be whoever you want to be. It all comes down to you and the choices you make. Faith, self-love, digging deep and pushing against all odds, will help get you to the next level. You can change your own life by empowering or allowing yourself to be empowered to become the best you. Take Sophia's advice and find positivity in any situation no matter how bad it may be. What if Vicky hadn't seen the positive in her mother's comments when she was only a little girl? Challenges or struggles are for building your resilience. It is when you push through them, get over them and use them as steppingstones, that you truly grow; move to the next level. Twins Emily and Allison demonstrate through their journey that life goes beyond being comfortable where you are by taking on new challenges that fall outside of their comfort zone. By learning, healing and growing, you can too become an Impactor, bringing hope and positivity to the world.

Founders of The Next Impactors

LOREN MICHAEL HARRIS   **JEFF LEVIN**

Loren and I made a connection mid-summer of 2018. Jeff, just finished up raising 1 million meals for Food Insecure Children in the Chicagoland area & Loren Harris was about to begin one of the most powerful inner-city, underprivileged mentoring programs to ever hit Chicago and beyond – The Power of We Symposium. Loren wanted to honor us as the only for-profit company, doing "non-profit like work, amongst other non-profits being featured on the evening. Following the Power of We, later in the fall, we got together one evening over Lou Malnati's Pizza to talk. We talked about how we can further join forces to collaborate, and the soon to be famous question was posed. "What if we created a reality show that highlighted people spreading positive, impactful messages and missions of hope throughout the globe?" That night – we brainstormed to the wee hours of the morning on the back of a napkin – literally a Lou Malnati's napkin and the next day we went to work. In less than one month, we assembled 5 talented celebrity judges who believed so much in the concept of the show. They were willing to not only serve as judges but also donate over $500,000 in prizes to the winner of the First Next Impactor Competition – crowned on August 30th, 2019.

It is our dream to syndicate The Next Impactor Globally & flood the airways with a new standard for entertainment. One that spreads service, impact, hope, and positivity from everyday ordinary people that believe their lives can make a significant impact on the communities their lives were made to perfectly serve. So to think, it all began over a slice of pizza. Just goes to show that when two or more gather in his name amazing, unheard of things happen. An Impactor is a world changer. Next Impactor with the help of our platform, will change the world. – Jeff & Loren.

About the Author

Vicky Omifolaji is the owner of Vicky Omifolaji Consulting & Psychotherapy Services with over 20 years' experience helping and empowering people to deal with their life issues.

She is also the Director of Life Skills Programs for Young People, an organization with the primary goal of helping to develop critical life skills in children as well as young adults. These include the skills to believe in themselves, handle their feelings, make and keep friends, cooperate with others, foster respect, and resolve a conflict which in turn builds resilience.

Vicky also makes herself available for private and corporate speaking events. She organizes events to help foster solid relationships, such as Valentine's Day bash, Mother and daughter high tea events and ladies' retreat.

She is an author of children's (picture) books to help in equipping children with skills including bully proofing, anger management, problem-solving and emotional self-awareness.

Vicky has made it her life's mission to help others with her wisdom and empathy. She is down to earth and tries to impact everyone that crosses her path positively.

Happily married to Dr. Stephen Omifolaji, they have three wonderful children – Shina, Victor, and Lola.